John Mortimer

Samples from the Note Books of an Uncommercial Traveller

John Mortimer

Samples from the Note Books of an Uncommercial Traveller

ISBN/EAN: 9783337205034

Printed in Europe, USA, Canada, Australia, Japan

Cover: Foto ©Andreas Hilbeck / pixelio.de

More available books at **www.hansebooks.com**

SAMPLES

FROM THE NOTE BOOKS
OF
AN UNCOMMERCIAL TRAVELLER.

Reprinted from the "Diary and Buyers' Guide,"
1898.

MANCHESTER:
PALMER, HOWE AND CO.,
PRINCESS STREET.

PREFATORY NOTE.

THE following pages are reprinted from the "Diary and Buyers' Guide" for 1898, issued by Henry Bannerman & Sons Limited, Manchester.

Under the title of "*Samples from the Note Books of an Uncommercial Traveller*" some miscellaneous sketches of a recreative kind are here submitted which may, perhaps, be found not altogether devoid of interest. In this connection the author thinks it necessary to say that, in order to adapt them to special uses, the original notes have, for the most part, been considerably abbreviated and modified, and in some cases must be regarded as little more than pegs upon which to hang pictorial illustrations.

CONTENTS.

	PAGES
ROUND YORK MINSTER ...	1–11
A JOURNEY TO SOUTH WALES ...	12–39
JOHN VAREY'S CASH-BOOK ...	40–60
A NOTE ON NOTTINGHAM ...	61–73
RYE AND WINCHELSEA ...	74–80
YARMOUTH TO BARMOUTH ...	81–105
TUNBRIDGE WELLS ...	106–114
SOME COMMERCIAL TRAVELLERS' SAMPLES:—	
I.—A DANTZIC TRAVELLER'S REPORTS ...	115–118
II.—THE ADVENTURES OF JOHN KIGHLEY ...	119–145
III.—"A VETERAN HIGHWAYMAN" ...	146–152
IV.—A BOOK OF RHYMES ...	153–155
IN THE NORTH COUNTRY ...	156–167
A DAY AT DERBY ...	168–184

ILLUSTRATIONS.

	PAGE
BOOTHAM BAR AND THE MINSTER, YORK ...	... FRONTISPIECE.
STONEGATE, YORK ...	... *facing* 4
SHAMBLES, YORK ...	,, 6
MICKLEGATE BAR, YORK ...	,, 10
EASTGATE STREET, CHESTER ...	,, 12
OLD MANSIONS IN BRIDGE STREET, CHESTER	,, 13
OLD SHOPS IN THE ROWS, CHESTER ...	,, 16
ENGLISH BRIDGE, SHREWSBURY	,, 17
MARKET SQUARE, SHREWSBURY...	,, 18
HIGH STREET, SHREWSBURY ...	,, 19
THE QUARRY, SHREWSBURY ...	,, 20
HEREFORD CATHEDRAL AND BRIDGE ...	,, 21
SWANSEA ...	23
MUMBLES ...	,, 26
TENBY HARBOUR ...	,, 28
ST. DAVIDS ...	,, 30
SPECIMEN PAGES OF JOHN VAREY'S CASH-BOOK ...	*page* 43
NOTTINGHAM CASTLE ...	... *facing* 64
MARKET PLACE, NOTTINGHAM. ...	... ,, 65
LONG ROW, NOTTINGHAM...	... ,, 66
TRENT BRIDGE, NOTTINGHAM ...	,, 68
RYE ...	,, 76
MERMAID STREET, RYE ...	,, 77
WINCHELSEA ...	,, 78
LINCOLN ...	,, 81
STONEBOW, LINCOLN ...	... ,, 83
BOSTON CHURCH ...	... *between* 88 and 89
BARGATE GREEN AND CHURCH, BOSTON	,, 88 ,, 89
KING'S LYNN ...	,, 88 ,, 89

ILLUSTRATIONS—Continued.

	PAGE
*Market Place, East Dereham	between 88 and 89
Market Place, Yarmouth	facing 94
Yarmouth	,, 95
Ely	,, 98
View on the River, Cambridge	,, 99
Stamford	between 104 and 105
Lichfield Cathedral	,, 104 ,, 105
Barmouth	,, 104 ,, 105
The Pantiles, Tunbridge Wells	facing 111
Fac-simile Page of a portion of the Dantzic Traveller's Report relating to Manchester Merchants	page 117
Fac-simile Page of John Kighley's Journal relating to his Captivity in France	,, 123
Fac-simile Page of John Kighley's Journal relating to his American Journeys	,, 141
Kirkby Stephen	acing 160
Barnard Castle	,, 161
Market Place, Barnard Castle	,, 162
Richmond, Yorkshire	,, 166
Market Place, Richmond	,, 167
Near Miller's Dale	page 170
Market Place, Derby	facing 170
On the Derwent, Old Silk Mill, Derby	,, 174
All Saints' Church, Derby	,, 176
Saw Mills—Carriage and Wagon Dept., Midland Railway Works	between 182 and 183
Machine Shop ,, ,, ,, ,, ,, ,,	,, 182 ,, 183
Erecting Shop—Locomotive Department ,, ,, ,,	,, 182 ,, 183

* *The View of East Dereham referred to in the text being found unavailable the present one has been substituted for it.*

SAMPLES

FROM THE NOTE BOOKS OF AN UNCOMMERCIAL TRAVELLER.

ROUND YORK MINSTER.

I RAN down the other day to look again upon old Eboracum, a city associated with many pleasant and far-dated recollections. Some notes of these recollections, relating to a visit made more than twenty years ago, I have before me now. Comparing old things with new, I find it there recorded that "the railway station is just inside the walls, and the trains run in and out along the iron roadway through an open gateway formed by a graceful Tudor arch." On this later occasion I alighted from the train to find myself set down outside the walls, and in a station of vast proportions, with broad and spacious platforms, overarched by four wide-spanned, manygirdered roofs of iron and glass of wonderful curvature of form, and supported by rows of massive pillars, adorned with capitals of classic mould. York is a city whose architectural attractions are mainly of the Gothic kind, but more remotely than these there were buildings of Roman construction, an emperor's palace among the rest. In view of such historic facts it is, therefore, perhaps not incongruous that, in selecting a style, the builders of this new station, and the handsome hotel which forms a portion of it, should have adopted the Italian, especially too as in obtaining their deep foundations they had to dig into a vast Roman cemetery to the disturbance of the remains of some thousands of departed Romans deposited there in urns, coffins of wood and stone, and other forms of sepulture.

As soon as you have crossed the station threshold, passing outwards, the old-world charm of York is made manifest, for there, in front of you, cresting the green embankment, is the grey limestone wall which marks, on this side, the city's ancient boundary. From this wall, when you have gained access to it near by, you may look over a wavy expanse of roofs of purple slate and red pantiles, broken by church towers and spires, with the great Minster rising grandly over all, "lifting from out the populous city grey cliffs of lonely stone into the midst of sailing birds and silent air." The way citywards lies fair and picturesque before you—with the Minster towers in view—leading past a green enclosure, the burial place of cholera victims in years long gone, and so to the bridge of Lendal, a product of the iron age, contrasting in its graceful Tudor arch with that older triple-arched stone one lower down the river, visible from here and known as Ouse bridge. A fair, broad stream is the Ouse, as viewed from the bridges, with pleasant outlooks up and down it, showing here at Lendal old towers on either side marking the terminations of the city walls, and, on its banks, irregular lines of buildings, prominent among them being the ancient river front of the Guildhall. Close by Ouse bridge, where waterlanes run down to the river, you have the King's staith and the Queen's staith, and other wharfages, with little clusters of masts where barges are moored, for the Ouse is navigable to the sea. Among one's agreeable recollections in this connection is a voyage along it to the city from Selby, a dozen miles away. For the riverside loiterer, too, there are pleasant walks along the banks, such as the broad Esplanade here at Lendal, or that tree-shaded one beyond Ouse bridge, where you have a fine avenue of elms -still known as the New Walk, though in reality an ancient promenade which has been trodden by many generations of the citizens of York.

Leaving the bridge of Lendal, you pass by the grounds which contain the ruined abbey of St. Mary, and, taking that direction, along a well-kept thoroughfare, soon find yourself in the cathedral close. The houses at one time reached to the Minster walls, as they do in continental towns, but a space has been cleared—paved on one side and with fresh green grass and trees on the other. It is not to one's purpose to describe the cathedral. That has been done already in various forms, and a guide book will tell you all you require to know, but as you look up at the west front you may remember that Ruskin has spoken contemptuously of its towers as "eight pinnacled things which are mere confectioner's Gothic." However that may be, to use words of his own, the special application of which one has forgotten, it is pleasant in front of such a piece of architecture "to look up at the deep-pointed porches and the dark places between the pillars, where there were statues once, and where the fragments, here and there, of a stately figure are still left, and so higher and higher up to the great mouldering wall of rugged sculpture and confused arcades shattered and grey and grisly, with heads worn by the rain and swirling winds into yet unseemlier shapes, and coloured by the deep russet orange lichen, and so higher still to the bleak towers, so high above that the eye loses itself among the bosses of the traceries."

On this journey I content myself with a brief survey of the cathedral's interior; but referring to my notes of an earlier visit, I find it there recorded how on

STONEGATE, YORK.
(From a Photograph by Messrs. F. Frith & Co. Ltd. By permission.)

that occasion I passed with something like awe along the mighty pillared nave, and reached the choir as the verger threw open the gate for morning service, and how that courteous functionary conducted me to a richly-canopied stall, one of many ranged on each side of the choir, and in close proximity to one with the word "Stillington" carved on it, suggesting memories of Lawrence Sterne, sometime vicar of that place and prebendary of York. There I sat in my stall, and in the softened light that came through a magnificent east window heard, during the service, an anthem gloriously sung to the accompaniment of a mighty organ, whose—

> Thunder music rolling shook
> The prophets blazoned on the panes.

If you wish to obtain a lofty point of observation you may ascend the great central tower and look down through a blue veil of smoke upon the city clustered below, and mark the thin grey line of the ancient wall and the broken space through which the river flows, and, beyond the wall, the houses straggling out irregularly to the green fields, and further away, studded with towns and hamlets, the great vale of York stretching away to the east and west hills.

In the cathedral precincts there is much to interest one in a quiet, restful way, and many quaint presentations of architecture, domestic and other, present themselves to the observing eye. Here, for instance, is an old building with a projecting story supported by quaintly carved wooden figures, and surmounted by a steep overhanging roof of red pantiles. Through an archway, with a heavy, nail-studded door, you enter and find yourself in a paved quadrangle with the same steep roofs and projecting stories as without. In the upper story are diamond-paned windows, some of them open and gay with flowers, and on the opposite side is a corresponding archway leading to a broad staircase. On a former visit, as I wandered about guideless, I asked a little fellow the name of the place, and he told me lispingly that it was "Taint Tillum's Tollit," which I found out afterwards meant St. William's College. This was formerly the residence of the cathedral clergy, founded for that purpose by Edward IV. Here, in 1642, Charles I. set up a printing press and commenced a paper war against his enemies, which soon after resulted in a real one. A little beyond the college, at the corner of the narrow street which bears that name, in what was then a small dark shop, Hudson, the railway king, sold drapers' wares before he entered upon those daring speculations which, in their temporary and brilliant success, furnished Carlyle with the materials for that satire known among his *Latterday Pamphlets* as "Hudson's Statue." Before leaving the region of things ecclesiastical, it may be said that what strikes a stranger very forcibly in York is the number of old

SHAMBLES, YORK.
(From a Photograph by Messrs. F. Frith & Co. Ltd. By permission.)

churches crowded within the walls, each one a storehouse of interesting materials for the antiquary. More than a score of them are at present in existence, but there used to be upwards of forty. You come upon them continually in all sorts of odd corners and in the quaintest forms of Gothic architecture, some with steeples, others with towers, it may be of Norman build and roofed with pantiles, and others again without steeples or towers. One of the churches is said to be built on the site of a temple of Diana, and from the steeple of another they used to hang out a lantern to guide travellers by night through the forest of Galtres.

Passing out of College Street you come upon Goodramgate, which is as old as the Danish occupation, that famous warrior, Guthrum, having dwelt in it. It is from the Danish "Yorvak," by the way, that we have derived the modern name of York. In like manner as you thread your way among the streets, or rather gates as they are mostly called, you note that the city's history is recorded in some sort by their names. Quaint, too, are many of them in their domestic architecture, showing curious carved gables, high peaked roofs, overhanging fronts, and other mediæval characteristics. One little reminder of a bygone time one has met with in the shape of a large extinguisher, placed beside a door, serviceable for extinguishing the light in the days of link boys and sedan chairs. Old hostelries there are, too, in these streets with associations clinging to them of the days of mail coaches and post horses. A typical street of the old-fashioned order is Stonegate, with its old-world buildings and shops, where you can buy old books, old pictures, old china, old silversmiths' ware, and antique survivals of many other kinds. The quaintest street of all perhaps is that known as the Shambles, narrow, pent-in, and eminently picturesque, given up mainly to butchers and representative of the time when the trades and crafts located themselves in special thoroughfares, traceable still by the names they bear. In contrast with the narrow Shambles is the broad Pavement, into which it emerges at the point which marks the demolished church of St. Crux. Here one's eye lights upon a gabled building, which was once a mansion but is now a draper's shop, and noticeable on the wall is a small tablet recording the fact that here in 1606 was born Sir Thomas Herbert, a notable man in many ways, and who was with Charles I. on the scaffold, and wrote an interesting account of his execution. In the neighbourhood of this Pavement, and the broad, spacious area of Parliament Street adjoining it, the market folk congregate, and if you are here on a market day you will have a refreshing sense of mingling with stalwart, broad-shouldered farmers, sons of the soil, whose north country speech falls pleasantly upon the ear, and who bring with them into the market place a sense of the country green. In the summer season, too, as you thread your way among the multitudinous stalls that crowd the space in Parliament Street, you will find it fragrant with fruits and flowers from Yorkshire gardens and orchards. This market place of York, with its agricultural and pastoral associations, is always attractive to one who remembers how once upon a time he journeyed to it from Crayke on an early summer morning, along fourteen miles of road in a slow-moving covered market wagon, and in company with market folk as interesting in their way as those travellers of the same type whom Thomas Hardy has described in his Wessex tales.

If, from the market place you pass along High Ousegate and some further thoroughfares, you will be in the neighbourhood where, we are told, the old-time drapers had their shops, a locality not forsaken of them yet. In these and similar other thoroughfares, such as Coney Street, Spurriergate, and the rest, there is—in the shops that line them, the people on the footpaths, and the vehicular traffic—an unmistakable air of the county town, not without a certain sedateness, but bright and cheerful in its expression. To the stranger who has come from a manufacturing town the influence of such surroundings is acceptable, he feels that he is beyond the region of mill chimneys, for in the city of York it is not calico they manufacture but confectionery, their reputation in that direction being wide spread and of ancient date. Cattle and corn also, among things agricultural, prevail largely as products marketable here. York, however, has not been without its claims to be considered a mercantile city, having still its Companies of Merchant Adventurers and Merchant Tailors, survivals of the old Trade Guilds, with two ancient halls remaining to serve as habitations for them. Somewhat removed from such trading streets as one has been traversing, and at the end of Castlegate is the great walled space which contains within it Her Majesty's prison, known as York Castle, and the remains of the more ancient stronghold. Clifford's tower, rising picturesque and grey from the summit of a green and tree-planted mound, is suggestive of that terrible self-immolation, and accompanying massacre, of many Jews and their families who had sought refuge in it from their persecutors in Cœur de Lion's time, a gruesome story as related by the local historians. Of a former visit one has the recollection of climbing to the summit of this tower and seeing there a flourishing walnut tree, which some say George Fox the Quaker planted when a prisoner there.

Judging from the names of its thoroughfares, York would seem to have been a city of many gates, but that term as applied to them was probably derived from the Danish *gada*, which meant a street. The real gateways here are known as Bars, and nowhere

MICKLEGATE BAR, YORK.

else has one seen such well preserved specimens as the four existing ones, known respectively as Walmgate, Monk, Micklegate, and Bootham, delightful to the eye of the antiquarian in their towered loftiness and embattled and turreted picturesqueness. A visit to York would be incomplete without a perambulation of its walls and an inspection of these remarkable gateways. At Micklegate Bar—seen once to wonderful advantage when, on the occasion of a military display, soldiers of horse and foot were passing in parallel lines through its arched ways—one's survey of the city is brought to an end. This Bar commanded the approach from London, and it was here that the heads of traitors and prisoners of war were placed. Upon its summit, after the battle of Wakefield, was stuck the head of that Richard, Duke of York, of whom, in *Henry IV.*, Shakespere makes the haughty Queen Margaret say—

> Off with his head and set it on York gates,
> That York may look upon the town of York.

In the waning summer afternoon, my pilgrimage ended, I leave the city with the sunshine sleeping on its grey old spires and towers, its time-honoured streets, and its broad river flowing through, changeful yet changeless, as it has done through the centuries, though Roman, Saxon, Dane and Norman have come and left upon its banks the traces of their lives in memorial names and mouldering stones.

A JOURNEY TO SOUTH WALES.

IN the Autumn of a year now remote the present writer started out, along with other travellers, on a journey to Tenby, the intention being not only to make the acquaintance of that attractive watering place, but to see something of the country which lies along that portion of the Welsh coast. The holiday was a brief one, somewhat resembling a swallow's flight in its glancing swiftness, but in setting down the record of it one is tempted to adopt a more leisurely form of progress, as far as the outward journey is concerned, and avail one's self of the opportunity to weave into the narrative some impressions, gained at other times and seasons, of places which were passed on the way.

Our route lay through Chester, but we only got such a passing view of old Caerleon by Dee side as could be obtained from the lofty railed way which skirts the Roodee and crosses the famous river. But Chester is

EASTGATE STREET, CHESTER.

OLD MANSIONS IN BRIDGE STREET, CHESTER

not a city to be passed in that flying fashion. To the
dweller in Cottonopolis it is particularly attractive by
reason of the contrast it affords—in its restful repose
and grave antiquity—to the busy, bustling conditions
of his own mercantile and manufacturing surroundings.
It is for him the nearest city which retains intact its
ancient walls, and as he makes the circuit of them it
is with a new sensation that he paces the raised footway, extending for nearly two miles between parapets,
and looks out upon things old and new within and
without the boundaries; clustered roofs with a haze of
smoke about them, and rising above these the massive
square-towered cathedral and the castle showing warm
colour in the ruddiness of the prevailing red sandstone;
lines of buildings, presenting many quaint features in
their picturesque irregularity, visible when you come
to some gateway commanding a main thoroughfare;
the river, too, busy with gay aquatic life, mainly of
the pleasure-seeking kind, where the stream flows by
the green slopes of Grosvenor Park and the grove-
shaded walks, where are the boats and the boathouses.
Hereabouts you come upon the weir and the water-
mills and see the bridges, and, at a lower point, the
low-lying Roodee or Roodeye, with the posts and rails
of the racecourse track clearly outlined on the broad
grassy spaces, from which the ground rises terraced
and amphitheatre-like round the great part of it.
Upon these and many other things does the stranger

look, getting at times views beyond them, on the one hand over great spaces of Cheshire landscape, or on the other to where "the distant mountains rise above the fair green fields of Wales."

Nor, when he has descended to lower levels, can he fail to be deeply interested in the shop architecture, which is of the quaintest kind, for here are the famous "Rows" where many of the tradesmen have their shops, the arrangement of which is almost unique. What a visitor sees as he passes by one of these Rows is a line of shop fronts in the basement with an open space above them, over which, often supported on stone pillars, the rest of the buildings are raised, showing frequently sharply-gabled, steep-roofed fronts with black and white ornamentation and quaint carving on the woodwork. Here and there, however, in this lower line of shops, the visitor comes upon little stairways which lead him to the roofs above, and then he finds himself on another raised and covered footway, balustraded, and with another line of shops recessed there, suggestive of a kind of cloistered seclusion in their withdrawal from the rude traffic of the street below. Here in these long rows, sheltered from the weather, it is possible to go a shopping however showery the day may be. How it came about that such a style of building was adopted the antiquarian finds himself unable to say. One evidence of their remote origin is the existence, under some of them, of crypts or vaulted chambers, showing curiously groined roofs and other remains of a remote early English architecture. Though, in modern building, the rows are not being repeated, it is interesting to note that in many cases the quaint features of the earlier times are being maintained in gabled fronts and carved ornamentation.

From Chester we rattled along, at express speed, until we came to Shrewsbury. We always like to halt at Shrewsbury when there is a chance, though on this occasion it was only to dine. Like Chester, there is a fine old flavour about the place with its varied historical associations and lingering ancientry. This is in evidence as soon as you have passed outwards from the busy railway station, for there above you on high ground is the castle, a great towered and battlemented pile of red sandstone, restored for the most part, but retaining within it portions of the stronghold which was erected in 1070 by the first Earl of Shrewsbury, Roger de Montgomery, a warrior who also founded an abbey here and died a monk. They show you what is regarded as his effigy carved in stone and lying there in the Abbey Church, another venerable pile of red sandstone, rich in Norman and later forms of architecture, and which you reach by crossing the English Bridge which spans the Severn. There, too, in that quarter may you note how "the old order changeth yielding place to new," for near by the church in a goods yard of the railway type given up to the storage of drain pipes and other forms of pottery, you may see a beautifully carved stone pulpit, reminiscent of monastic uses. Shrewsbury is a town of many churches, grey and spired or towered, some of them reaching back in their foundation to remote dates, notably in the case of St. Mary's, a beautiful building, famous, among other adornments, for its "painted windows richly dight." The antiquity of the streets, too, is apparent as soon as you set foot in the town. Turning from the Castle along a main thoroughfare which bears that name, you get sight of the grey old walls of the famous Grammar School, standing back within a green enclosure. It is a school rich in traditions of eminent scholars who have passed through it, Sir Philip Sydney being among the earlier ones, and it is interesting to know that it was founded by Edward VI. at the solicitation of two worthy men, one of them being Hugh Edwards, a mercer. It is no longer a school, its masters and scholars having found a new home on the brow of a hill overlooking the Severn, but it is still devoted to educational purposes of the free library and museum types, and if you climb the stone stairway, up and down which so many youthful feet have passed, and look through the old rooms, you will find memorials of former uses in the names of departed scholars freely carved in the woodwork of the window spaces.

OLD SHOPS IN THE ROWS, CHESTER.

cloth and flannels, "of which great quantities were bought in the town and sent abroad." They have known something of the cotton manufacture, too, but when Lancashire competition proved too strong the industry had to be abandoned. The linen manufacture also has been cultivated here, retaining its hold longer than the other. They have been fighting people too, these proud Salopians, and they have done honour to warriors, as you will see, by placing a statue of Lord Clive in the market square, and one of Lord Hill lifted high on a mighty column in the Abbey Foregate. Of that renowned knight Sir John Falstaff you will find no memorial, though he did stoutly maintain that on a famous battlefield close by he had "fought a long hour by Shrewsbury clock."

One of the charming features of Shrewsbury is the River Severn which flows nearly round the town, almost islanding it, and leaving only a narrow neck of land at the point where you enter from the railway station. Pleasant it is to look down upon the stream from the bridge and see it flowing between green banks and osier-fringed islets, where the angler loves to moor his punt as he casts the alluring fly. Pleasanter still it is to wander along that part of the river from which, on the one side, you can see the town showing itself on the ridge along the line of the old wall with houses and gardens on the green slopes, and on the other the wooded height of Kingsland crowned by the

MARKET SQUARE, SHREWSBURY.

HIGH STREET, SHREWSBURY.

new Grammar School. Here, too, you come upon the famous Quarry-walk, and find yourself free to wander along avenues of magnificent limes such as you will rarely meet with elsewhere. One of these avenues runs by Severn side, and walking here you can watch the pleasure boats or racing craft glide by to the stroke of measured oars. Other avenues lead from the lower one to the town above, the intervening slopes being laid out so as to form a charming pleasure garden, and when you have reached the higher ground again you get views which reveal to you how beautiful are the surroundings of this delightful old town.

We must linger here no longer, however, but taking up our narrative again, go on to tell how, when we had left Shrewsbury behind us, we came in time upon Church Stretton, lying away there across the meadows on the right among the belts of fir plantations below the green-folded hills that rise in turfy undulations to the Long Mynd and the high moorlands, from which you can see far and wide over many counties. The line of the village street is distinguishable among the trees by the square tower of the church and the house roofs, over which the smoke rises slowly like a pale blue mist. It is one of the sweetest and quietest resting places with which we are acquainted. Across the valley to the left is the hill known as Caer Caradoc, with the remains of a British fort on its summit, where Caractacus made his last stand against the Romans. You reach it by a deep-grooved sandy lane, possibly following the track made by the ancient Britons to their stronghold. Further on we passed Ludlow, where we once lounged for a week-end, and on a sunny summer day got the keys of the castle and wandered about that fine old ruin at our own sweet will, seeing among other notable things the remains of the banqueting chamber where John Milton's *Masque of Comus* was first performed, and the chamber where Samuel Butler wrote part of *Hudibras*. The castle stands at an angle of the town, and shows itself boldly upon a high rock above a swan-haunted stream, and from its lofty towers you can look far away over the Welsh Marches. Then we slipped along through an orchard and hop-growing country to Hereford, memorable to us as a halting place in many journeys along the upper and lower Wye, for we have followed this river, in most of its windings, from Chepstow to Plynlimmon. The old city, as we have known it in leisurely loiterings about its neat and pleasant streets and in pilgrimages to its cathedral, is a place of pleasant memories. Here we have planned and started out on those memorable river rambles, and here too we have heard its chimes at night-time, ringing out into the quiet air the strains of some hope-inspiring psalm for wakeful ears. On its trading side the old town is associated with things refreshingly agricultural, with hops and malt, timber

THE QUARRY, SHREWSBURY.
(From a Photograph by Messrs. Valentine & Sons Ltd. By permission.)

HEREFORD CATHEDRAL AND BRIDGE.

and wool, oak bark and tanning, and with apple orchards and cider.

But here at Hereford we were, on this journey, forcibly reminded that—

> The best laid plans of mice and men
> Gang aft agley.

We had to change carriages, and in that movement a change came o'er the spirit of our Tenby dream. It was clear that there had been a mistake somewhere, for the guard of the train which took us forward declared that there was no chance of reaching Tenby that night, or indeed until Monday. If we were not going to Tenby, where were we going? That was the problem which required solving. The guard in his van turned the subject over in his mind, and came to us, when there was a chance, with suggestions and words of comfort. Finally we decided to take his advice and go with him to Swansea, and stay the week-end at the Mumbles. He seemed to have an instinctive knowledge of our tastes and desires, for he expressed regret that the coming darkness would shut out from our view some grand mountain scenery through which we had to pass. We had for fellow-passengers a quiet Welsh dissenting minister and a work-a-day iron-stained man, who was reading a society journal, and whom we supposed to be engaged on the railway, and to be returning home from his week's labour. He and the minister seemed to be known to each other. It turned out presently that these two had been companions on a longer journey than ours. They had travelled from somewhere out west in America, and after a stormy voyage across the Atlantic, were nearing their several destinations. The minister was returning from the search for health to his flock and home, and the worker in iron was making a sentimental journey to the friends and scenes of his youth. He had worked on this railway years ago, and could tell us a good deal about it and the scenes through which we were passing. They were an oddly-assorted couple, contrasting strongly in garb and speech; but it was pleasant to note the mutual respect they had for each other, and the sense of humour displayed by both. On we went, past pleasant Abergavenny, until the daylight was all gone, and lurid furnace fires gleamed out as we entered the iron country. These furnace lights sometimes flashed up from behind the mountains throwing out their rugged lines in black relief, the gloom and glare suggesting glimpses of an Inferno even to our iron-worker, though that was not the word by which he described it. We questioned him upon the daylight aspect of one of these valleys. "A one-horse, one-legged place," he said, "with wheels and rubbish, and general ugliness." On we rattled over the gloomy chasm spanned by the Crumlin Viaduct, where the multitudinous lights deep down below twinkled like fire-flies, and presently with " Good-bye,

1

SWANSEA.

Davis," "Good-bye, Griffiths," the minister dropped off at a junction, and the iron-worker was left. As we approached Aberdare, he stood up in the carriage and looked earnestly out of the window. No one was expecting him, he said, but he would surprise them soon. " There it is," he exclaimed, " just as when I left it ; not a bit different." He was hardly able to tell in the uncertain light whether Aberdare was changed or not ; but his heart seemed to go out to it, and it was a joy to him to find the town standing where it did. We bade him a cordial good-bye, and hoped he would receive the welcome he looked for.

A broad gas-lighted street of shops and houses, with whitened fronts and flagstaffs projecting from them like barbers' poles, a street so filled with a busy Saturday-night crowd that we found it best to walk in the roadway up and down which the tram-cars glided, these, with a variously-derived sense of being in a seaport, make up the impressions left upon us of Swansea. Very slight impressions truly for so large and important a town, the aspect of which, over a wider area, will be better gained from the illustration here given. We were only birds of passage in this case, however, and time and we were on the wing. The last train and the last tram-car had left, so there was nothing for it but to hire a cab, and in this unsentimental fashion we made our way along five miles of the margin of Swansea Bay to the

Mumbles. In the doubtful light the road, the trees, the sandhills, and the shore all wore a dusty white appearance; presently we passed between whitened houses and pulled up opposite a whitened garden wall and read the name of our hotel on a lamp over a gateway festooned with trailing greenery. Somehow, when we had entered it, this inn, with its many staircases and passages, its quaint bow-window in the bar filled with warm light and its French windows opening from the sitting-rooms to the little garden space fronting the road filled with shrubs and ferns and rock-work, made us think persistently of Dickens. There were strains of music and other festive signs about, and we found that there had been some sports, and that the fishing lads and their lasses were dancing in an upper chamber.

We went to rest with a sense of disappointment that we were not at Tenby, and with a very vague notion of the sort of place to which the fates had willed that we should come. On the morrow, however, we found that we were at the extremity of a sharp curve of Swansea Bay, under a precipitous headland that terminates in three great masses of rock which project themselves seaward, with a lighthouse on the farthest point. Our inn was close upon the shore, and in front a fleet of eighty or more oyster smacks were tossing at anchor upon a turbulent tide, for it was blowing a gale and the wind, the mariners said, was on a lee shore.

Behind the inn there was a steep slope of sheep-clipped down with the limestone cropping out of it. Beyond the inn, looking towards Swansea, the ground sloped more gently and was covered with gardens and white houses, and there was a church with a square tower and beyond that the ruins of a Norman castle. If we knew anything of geology we might say something about this wonderful rock wall, which forms the headland known as the Mumbles. Nowhere have we seen limestone, red sandstone, and what appear to be igneous rocks jumbled together in such wild confusion. We climbed to the down above to taste the delight of wrestling with the mighty wind that was sweeping over it with almost hurricane strength, and before which it was scarcely possible to stand upright. We could see the vast sweep of the bay outlined with faint blue uplands and fringed at the water's edge with the white foam of the breakers. Copper smelting, iron-working Swansea was in sight, toned down by distance to a hazy area of chimneys and a haunting cloud. We found that in some great convulsion of nature the headland on which we were standing had been rent in twain, and a deep, yawning chasm or ravine had been formed in the red sandstone. We crept down out of the wind among the scattered masses of rock that had fallen into the gulf. There was a narrow opening seaward, and through it we got, as in a framed picture, a view of a strip of the shore and sea and the distant coast. It was a wild-looking place that gave one a sense of the possibility of those red walls snapping to again and burying one out of sight.

In such a loitering fashion we rambled on behind the lighthouse point and Mumbles Head to the steep gorse-clad margin of Bracelet Bay, and lay down in a sheltered nook and feasted our eyes "upon the wideness of the sea." Then we returned to our inn to eat oysters, as was most fitting in a place known also as Oystermouth; and later visited the castle, and lounged about the shore.

On the morrow, though the storm had not altogether subsided and the waves were still high, it was proposed by the adventurous spirits of the party that we should charter one of those oyster smacks seen tossing there upon the tide, and make for Tenby, instead of going there by rail. After some discussion, the adventurous ones had their way. Most of the boats had hoisted sail, and were off oyster dredging, but a few remained. A skipper was found willing to undertake the task; and after much going to and fro about the beach, and consultation with our ancient mariner, the needful preparations were declared complete. Two other mariners had been found to man the craft, provisions had been laid in in the shape of some hard ship biscuits, another traveller had been added to the number of voyagers, and finally we and our luggage were put into a frail looking little boat and launched

MUMBLES.

through the breakers. At once we shipped a heavy sea, and found ourselves sitting with our feet deep in salt water. The luggage had come to grief, and had to be hoisted above high-water mark. Someone suggested that we might have to swim, which was pleasant to the only man of the party who couldn't. Eventually we made our vessel and scrambled over the side, and with many a "Ho! ho! Ha! ha! Yeave ho!" the anchor was weighed, and the brown sails hoisted and filled to the breeze, and we were tacking about in the bay. It was a rough kind of craft, with very low bulwarks, and deck strewn with chains, ropes, spars, and dredging materials. The luggage was stowed in the hold, and we had to lie about where we could, shifting constantly as the navigation of the vessel required, but generally finding ourselves on the side which was drenched with the waves. We were a long time in the bay, and seemed to make no headway. Whereupon we ventured to ask the skipper when we should clear the point. "Presently," he said, "but there is a nasty jump to be made," which meant we were going to run with a race of the tide through a narrow gut and over a reef, which at low water connects the lighthouse rock with the mainland. We were beginning to sympathise with Gonzalo, in the *Tempest*, when he said: "Now would I give a thousand furlongs of sea for an acre of barren ground, long heath, brown furze, anything. The wills above be done! but I would fain die a dry death." However, we held our breath and said no more until that jump had been made and we were out in the open. If we had been a little more comfortable in that rude craft, and among those troubled waters, perhaps we might have felt some of the sentiment which clings around a fishing boat, and lends to it an idealistic charm. Perhaps we might have speculated upon what is meant by the "singing in the sails which is not of the breeze," or have felt the delight of a wind that "sweeps a music out of sheet and shroud." Perhaps we realised most that our boat's effort was "to war with that living fury of waters, to bare its breast moment after moment against the unwearied enmity of ocean, the subtle, fitful, implacable smiting of the black waves provoking each other on endlessly, all the infinite march of the Atlantic rolling on behind them to their help, and still to strike them back into a wreath of smoke and futile foam and win its way against them, and keep its charge of life from them." On we went keeping sight of the shore, past Oxwich Bay and Port Eynon Bay, all the land seeming asleep as we sailed by. It was a fine coast, with long spaces of level sand, and pleasant uplands, with grand rock scenery, as at Port Eynon Point, round which we came in sight of the wonderful mass of piled-up crags called Worms Head, whither came many artists, as the man at the helm told us. As the afternoon wore on we entered Carmarthen Bay,

two youths came to our rescue, and skilfully pulled us through the shallows to the harbour steps. They had just towed in a derelict boat with an oar in it and bits of tree branches for rowlocks. It was a relic of the storm, and possibly, if it could have spoken, might have had some sad story of shipwreck to tell.

Tenby consists of a rocky promontory between two bays. On the seaward point there is a great crag, honeycombed with wonderful sea caves; a zigzag staircase is cut in the rock, and on its summit is a fort. This is St. Catherine's. Farther away to the right is Caldey Island. The bays have beautiful reaches of the smoothest sand, and the seawall consists of precipitous cavernous rocks. The houses are terraced or clustered picturesquely upon the promontory, and the limit of the old town is marked by a grey moss-grown wall, with the remains of towered gateways. Our hotel was the Royal Gatehouse, occupying, we imagine, the site of one of the gates, and placed on the highest point of the High Street. As we sat at meals we would look down over trees and rocks to the sail-dotted bay and harbour, and in clear weather sixteen miles away to Worms Head. We found that we were there out of season, the fashionable crowd had fled, and the town, as far as they were concerned, was as a banquet hall deserted. Yet it could hardly look more beautiful at any time than in the early morning when we strolled down to the quay

to chat with the skipper and his men who had slept on board their boat and were talking of going round to Stackpole to dredge for oysters if the sea would calm itself a little. We had the castle hill with its gravelled walks and smooth-shaven grass, the shore, and the caves pretty nearly all to ourselves. The town lay behind us clearly defined in the bright sunlight against a sky of sapphire. Along the sandy shore, on rock and island and crested wave, there were wonderful delicate tints of colour that only an artist could describe. We loitered about the beach, lay down on the sand hills, to "watch the crisping ripples on the beach and tender curving lines of creamy spray," climed up and down rock stairways, lounged about the streets, and saw the picturesquely attired shrimp woman of Mr. Frith's picture which we saw at the Royal Institution before we came away. In the main street we noticed an inscription in black and red letters to the effect that in these cellars the Earl of Richmond, afterwards Henry VII., was hid after the battle of Tewkesbury. We went along the coast towards Saundersfoot over furze-clad combs that gave us glimpses of blue water between their green folds, reminding us of Devonshire, and through deep sandy lanes with high hedges and filled with ferns, to a glen that runs down between dripping barnacled rock walls, to a shore where the waves have left myriads of beautiful shells and pebbles. Then we went to our inn and dined, and after that, though the moon and stars were shining brightly over the castle and cliff and bay, of all unlikely things amid so much beauty, we went to see the play.

Behind our hotel and connected with it was a little theatre, where they promised us the *Corsican Brothers*, as played at the Lyceum, London, and also a musical extravaganza called *Little Amy Robsart*. The tragedy, was an abbreviated addition, and rather failed in its effects upon us in spite of some most vigorous fencing and the praiseworthy efforts of the company generally. The extravaganza was better; it was full of fun and go, and there was a wonderful villain who brought down the house with a song, the burden of which was, " I shall never be happy again." In the intervals between the acts we were held in conversation by a gentleman next us, who looked like a backwoodsman, and wore a Tam-o'-Shanter bonnet, who talked transcendentalism, and had much to say about Gœthe and Schiller.

Next day it was decided that we should go to St. Davids. Taking train therefore, we ran along the coast, through a pleasantly varied county not very richly pastoral, and with just a suggestion of former wildness about it. We hadn't time to see Manorbier Castle, or the ruins of Lamphey Palace, or even to halt at Pembroke just then, but ran down to the dockyard among soldiers and sailors, and the busy stir of shipbuilding. Waiting upon the Admiralty Pier for the steam ferry to take us across to Neyland, we watched the building of the new ironclad *Ajax*.

> Wonderful for form and strength,
> Sublime in its enormous bulk.

From Neyland we ran up to Haverfordwest, a fine old town, picturesquely built on a hill-side, with a river running below, and the inevitable castle rearing its grey walls above the house roofs. We found that the whole district bristles with Norman castles; we could not move far without running against one. What struck us, too, was the English character of these towns. We were in Wales, but we heard no Welsh· spoken; justifying the old description of the country as Little England beyond Wales. Haverfordwest was *en fête*, if the visitation of a bishop could be so described. The streets and the inns were thronged with clergy. Robed figures with varied ecclesiastical head-gear flitted about the streets. There was a dark crowd of them gathered in the square before the Castle Hotel waiting for luncheon. We thought of Anthony Trollope and *Barchester Towers*, and would have liked to tarry among the crowd and note its different types; but we were hurrying from inn to inn to find a coach for St. Davids, a vehicle which was not to be found. There was a tall, contemplative police-constable standing in the main street, and with him we took counsel. St. Davids, he said, was sixteen miles away, and to reach it we must go over seventeen hills. A weary and undesirable road for walking, as it seemed to him. Nevertheless, after luncheon at the Salutation, we girded up our loins and started out. We passed from the fertile lowlands and fields, with the smoke of autumn fires in them, to a sterner and barer landscape, with a brown October look about it, dotted over with farmhouses and cottages with whitened walls and roofs, and bounded in the distance by a vague mountain line. Before the day was gone we passed Roch Castle, a solitary Norman tower on a rock, and got a sight of St. Bride's Bay. Presently we descended to the shore, and saw in the uncertain light a great black mass of rocks, and heard

> The plunging seas draw backward from the land.

Then we rose again inland, and plodded on doggedly and almost silently. At a point of the road where the darkness seemed impenetrable, and we were in doubt whether we hadn't taken a wrong turning, we suddenly descended into a deep hollow between hills and saw a group of white houses and the outline of a creek and boats, and heard the sound of falling water. It was pretty little Solva. The door of an inn stood invitingly open, the light of it streaming out into the dark. We were soon seated among other guests gathered about the cheerful fire in the clean spacious kitchen, a room with neat and orderly furniture and flowering plants in the window spaces. After resting for awhile, and discussing the refreshment set before us we passed out from Solva into the high country, and on between monotonous mud and stone fences until we saw the great sails of a windmill outlined against the sky, and shortly after reached St. Davids and our inn.

When we rose in the morning and went out to explore this strange old city by the sea, it seemed to us that the sharp sea wind and the cold grey sky were in keeping with the time and scene. We were in a wild remote country on a rocky headland—against which the great Atlantic waves break with all their fury—with a tract of sad, dull, melancholy fields stretching out behind. The houses, few in number, are of stone, whitened often over walls and roofs, and with bits of straggling garden greenery within whitened stone fences. Where the broad streets intersect each other is an open space and the remains of an ancient cross. Passing beyond this and through a ruined gateway we came to a rugged grey hollow of the land where stands the time-stained, weather-beaten old cathedral. A little stream winds through the hollow, and across it are the ivied ruins of Bishop Gower's palace, and on the slopes about are some clergy houses and groups of shattered trees that strain drearily from the sea. It has a strange, stern, enduring look this wild cathedral close, its limits marked out by remnants of walls and towers reared for its defence. One could not help contrasting it with some other cathedral closes, with their tall elms and cawing rooks and peaceful spaces of smooth grass. This ancient grey building, with its great square pinnacled tower in the centre, held together with bands of iron, is one of the oldest buildings of its kind in Britain. Workmen were restoring it, but there were still parts of it unroofed where "the grass blooms on the pavement and the sea wind chaunts among the ruined arches." Its foundations were laid in a far off time, possibly when Arthur and his knights were striving to "put down the heathen;" for St. David is said to have removed here from Caerleon early in the sixth century.

Leaving the cathedral, we wandered about the ruins of Bishop Gower's palace, and then took a post-chaise from our inn and drove back to Haverfordwest. Solva, with its creek and boats, and houses clustered in the hollow of the close-folding hills, lost none of its charms in the daylight; and, as we drove along within sight of St. Bride's Bay, we noted that there was much to remind us of the Devonshire combs, with the sea spaces visible between. As we drove into Haverfordwest, our old friend the policeman was standing in the same contemplative attitude in the same place as when we left.

Having rested for the night at the Salutation, if we had been asked whither we were bound next, our answer must have been that of Imogen, in *Cymbeline*, "To Milford Haven." We wonder if Shakespere was ever in Wales; we have always supposed that he had no actual experience of mountains, that "no mountain passions were to be allowed to him, that he had to be left with his king cups and clover pansies—the passing clouds—the Avon's flow, and the undulating hills and woods of Warwick." *Cymbeline* has the air of the mountains about it, whether Shakespere had any actual knowledge of them or not. Perhaps Milford Haven existed only for him as an unvisited place, and he may himself have asked with Imogen—

> Say how far it is
> To this same blessed Milford, and, by the way,
> Tell me how Wales was made so happy
> As to inherit such a haven.

Poor Imogen lost her way trying to find it; but we got there by train, and alighted at a little, dim-looking station. We passed up into the town, and from there saw the haven, beautiful in its wide expanse of almost land-locked waters, bounded with pleasant hills. There was a fine esplanade on the limestone cliff, and below it docks and shipping. There were rows of fine houses, and other evidences of great possibilities, which may some day be fulfilled.

Sir William Hamilton once owned this property, and when Nelson came to visit him he got the great admiral to lay the foundation stone of the church on the esplanade. After the battle of the Nile they brought here the royal mast-head of *L'Orient*—which was blown up on that occasion—and put it in the church to remind them of the great victory. After leaving Milford Haven, we rambled over a hill by green lanes, by beautiful wooded creeks, and along the shore of the haven, and crossing the little arm of it again at Neyland slipped down to the old town of Pembroke. We must not stay to talk about what we saw there more than to say that the most distinct picture we carried away was that of a long street with the castle at the end, and beneath it a group of huntsmen in scarlet coats and a moving pack of foxhounds. Then we went back to Tenby and rested the night, and on a glorious sunny morning started out for home. Skirting the shores of Carmarthen Bay we passed by many a castle and tower, and then plunged into the black country among the workers in coal and iron, and thence through the beautiful Vale of Neath, with its autumn-tinted woods clothing the mountain sides. From this we passed again through smiling sunlit Herefordshire and Shropshire, and halted once more at Shrewsbury.

It was Saturday night, and just dark as we walked up the Castle Street, for there is a certain old-fashioned pastrycook's shop there where they sell Shrewsbury cakes. The boys were crowding into the street from the great school, with all the impetuous delight of temporary freedom. It was a pleasant sight to see them hurrying along in groups and pairs. Into the pastrycook's came a tall jacketed lad to make some arrangements about a supper, for we heard the remark that it would take twenty minutes to boil the potatoes. It was a trifling incident, but somehow it impressed us more than much that we had seen in our holiday, and started us upon a long train of thought recalling *Tom Brown's Schooldays*, and those Rugby Saturday nights; and recalling, too, a remark of Tom's that "life is not all beer and skittles," which seemed to come very forcibly to us now that our short holiday was over, and we were going back again to be "nailed to the desk's dead wood."

JOHN VAREY'S CASH-BOOK.

WHEN John Milton said that "books are the precious life-blood of master spirits, treasured up on purpose to a life beyond life," he had no thought of a cash-book in his mind. Of all the books that a man might set himself to discourse upon none could be more unpromising than one which relates to cash. Such a volume savours not of immortality, in the literary sense, but rather of a transitory accountancy; figures are of the essence of its construction; debits and credits constitute the forms in which its dry facts are chronicled. Among many other kinds of books, I have had, and still have, a large acquaintance with cash-books—waste-books they are sometimes called in the phraseology of an antique book-keeping—and one's experience is that, in an ordinary way, these mercantile account books are not the kind of volumes from which one expects to extract much that is of literary or biographical interest. They are the despised and disregarded among books, not to be looked for upon stalls, or, if found there, and a man should turn the leaf, it will be but to close it again. John Varey's cash-book, however, is an exception in this regard, and may be taken as an evidence of the fact that there are cash-books and cash-books.

Regarding the personality of our author, let me say in the first instance that all I know of John Varey I have gleaned from this cash-book of his, which has been placed in my hands by Mr. Charles Roeder, a gentleman who, though of foreign birth, displays a greater amount of interest in local Lancashire lore, literary, social and antiquarian, than some upon whom such matters have naturally more immediate and legitimate claims. The manuscript, of which I have thus obtained temporary possession, is a faded-looking little volume in grey boards, and contains the personal accounts of its author duly recorded within columns ruled by himself on the blank pages, and representing a period extending from March 4, 1780, to January 2, 1786. The volume is evidently an odd one, belonging probably to a series, for it begins with a balance brought forward from an earlier book, and ends with a note of a similar transfer to a new one.

Regarding John Varey's book-keeping, it may be said that he had a style of his own; the transactions, whether debit or credit, follow each other consecutively, in a descriptive form, on the left-hand page, the amounts being separated into receipts and payments and duly arranged in the parallel columns on the opposite page, where there is ample space for marginal notes. John Varey's handwriting is marked by neatness, combined with a playful disposition to indulge occasionally in graceful little curves among the capital letters, but the effect of the whole is grave and sedate. His spelling is not always correct, but with a tendency to increased correctness as he proceeds with his journal. He sometimes indulges in variations of the same word, and it may be noted that he frequently spells the word "fent" thus, "ffent." To help him to a better knowledge of the language he is using we find that he possessed himself of an English Grammar, for which he tells us he paid Mr. Harrop one shilling and sixpence. Probably this Mr. Harrop was the well-known stationer, who had his shop in Market Place, Manchester, towards the close of last century. Being of a personal nature, the entries relate to the daily life of the chronicler, and possessing, as they do in this case, a peculiar quaintness, a precise fidelity, and even fulness of statement, and by virtue, moreover, of a certain illuminating quality of the narrative kind, which belongs rather to the diary than the cash-book, they become something more than merely barren debits or credits. We read between the written lines, and the figures become for us eloquent. When John

Dr Iohn Moss of his heirs

1750   Receipts   Paymts
July 5 Jnr Mary Moss for Clearing   Manchester   1 18 11 15 6½
     6 Debts to me the receipt is to   M Simmons   0 0 6
        Spencer in takeing care of   0 1 0
        Mr Graves Account
        Ere part to Manchester   — — —   0 0 1
        at Royal Oak to Mr Simmons   0 0 8
0 1 1   to Expences   0 0 11
0 7 2 10 paid Mr John Moses in   0 2 0
        full all the Money
        3 Guineas   0 1 0
        more at Moses returning   —   0 2 0
0 1 3½ pd a tankard bottle & Glass   0 3 0
        to Mrs [ ] Rowlings and Meals   3 17 0
        at Moss's   0 4 0
2 0 0   pd a Quires nothing
        paid Mr John Meyers
0 1 1½ Rd Blacker Coffin Cost   for a Coach   0 0 8
0 1 6   pd his Coffin for men   Easter   0 10 6
        pd Effing   Mary an 27{   17 10 0
1 1 6   Book Carr   Probate   —
        Land at   [ ]   0 1 0
        Long Stitch   0 1 2
                                                                        11 11 8   29 12 6

Varey, careful and painstaking man that he was, being anxious to give an accurate account to the minutest particular of the moneys that came into, or went out of, his possession, made his entries in this journal of his—a single item of a halfpenny being found not too insignificant for the record—he, doubtless, had no idea that the result would be subjected to a literary examination and audit when more than a century had elapsed. But so it has come about, and this bit of flotsam and jetsam caught in an eddy, and thence rescued from the tide which was bearing it down to destruction or oblivion, becomes interesting to us in ways speculative and suggestive.

One immediately attractive feature of the book is its local origin. It was written at Worsley, and we do not read far before discovering that the author was in the service of the great Duke of Bridgewater. Here at once is an interesting background for the central figure, whose outline it may afford us some recreation to shape from the recorded transactions, the small beer and other chronicles that go to make up his accounts. Like the life of man, John Varey's cash-book is rounded with a mystery—what preceded it or what followed after we know not. All that we know of the beginning and the end is that he makes his appearance upon the field of our mental vision with an entry to the effect that he "spent at John Mosse's 9d.," and he makes his exit with the statement that he "paid

B. Sothern for a gallon of rum 9s.," and so disappears from our view.

When John Varey made his first entry in his cash-book the Duke of Bridgewater, whom he served, would be about forty-five years of age, and had then completed his great canal-making scheme. Twenty years had elapsed since the first boat-load of coals was borne smoothly across the Barton aqueduct, and about eight years before this time the "Heart of Oak," a vessel of fifty tons burden, had passed down Neptune's stairway —as that chain of locks at Runcorn was called—the craft proceeding to Liverpool amid much rejoicing o the people who watched its progress. These smooth canals of the Duke's making were welcome additions to the means of travelling, for the roads in Lancashire were often rugged and bad, and the coach service of the scantiest kind. As we shall see from his chronicle, John Varey often availed himself of the Duke's waterways in his little local travels.

Regarding John Varey's service under the Duke, it may be said that an early entry in his cash-book is to the effect that on July 31st, 1780, he received of his Grace half-a-year's salary, amounting to £17. 10s., "due on the 29th May last." This item is suggestive, because it shows that John Varey's income from this source was a very modest one, and that the Duke was not a punctual paymaster. It would be rash, however, to conclude that the amount of the salary was a reliable indication of the character or the value of the services rendered for it. As we trace these payments we find that they are increased at intervals, until John Varey is in receipt of £60 per annum, paid in one sum, but it is noteworthy that there is always more or less delay in the settlement. All this is consistent with what we know of the canal-making Duke. What he might require of John Varey for £60 per annum we can only guess, seeing that he never paid the great engineer, Brindley, more than one guinea per week, and from 1765 to 1772 he paid him nothing at all. We know that when Brindley, being in great straits for want of money during that barren period, appealed to his Grace of Bridgewater, for whom he had done such marvellous work, he was met with the answer, "I am much more distressed for money than you; however, as soon as I can recover myself, your services shall not go unrewarded." Unrewarded, however, they did go, for Brindley died before the Duke found himself in a position to pay. All this is very interesting in view of the conditions under which recent canal-making has been conducted. The faithful but ill-used engineer had gone to his rest several years before John Varey made this first entry of salary in his book, and in the meantime the Duke's finances had no doubt improved, otherwise a longer period than two months might have elapsed between the due date and the settlement.

What was the exact nature of John Varey's duties, for which he received his thirty-five pounds per annum, is not quite clear. He may have been an under-steward, or have filled some similar position of trust. We find that—possibly for use in his occupation—he possesses himself of a case of drawing instruments, a parallel ruler, a square, and a Fenning's algebra. He moves about a good deal locally. There are frequent entries relating to expenses when engaged in selling beef for the Duke at Dixon Green and other neighbouring places, and he is occasionally commissioned to take sums of money to Manchester, in evidence of which we find that he spent sevenpence when "taking £75 to Mr. John Okell at Manchester on the Duke's account." Again, we come upon this entry, "Expenses at Manchester when I took Esqr. Rasbottom's, Esqr. Lowe's and Esqr. Lloyd's money on his Grace's account, one shilling." A more detailed statement relates to "Expenses in taking £600 to Mr. Tompkinson on his Grace's account." The expenditure on this occasion amounted to one shilling and a penny, and is thus particularised: "Turnpike to Manchester, 1d.; at Royal Oak with Mr. Tompkinson, 8d.; contingent expenses, 4d." In addition to this we find that he gives "To see the Irish giant in Manchester, 1s." It may be remarked here that probably this Mr. Tompkinson was the Duke's solicitor, of whom mention is made in Smiles' "Life of Brindley."

But it is not so much regarding his relations with the Duke that one gets up any interest in turning over the pages of John Varey's cash-book, for the references in that direction are vague and scanty. It is rather the man himself, his outward garb, his social relationships and surroundings, his pleasures and pursuits, as they are revealed to us in his simple, ingenuous book-keeping, that prove attractive to the extent of producing a feeling of friendly intimacy with him. The personality of an unknown author is always a matter of speculative curiosity to his readers. In John Varey's case he helps us unwittingly to a knowledge, and we get the impression of a man with a touch of quaint picturesqueness about him, a man withal who was as careful and precise in his exterior presentment as he was in his accounts. It would appear that after the fashion of his time he was a clean-shaven man, for we come upon payments for a razor, hone, razor strop and shaving soap. He wore his hair powdered, there being frequent entries relating to the purchase of that material, which cost him sometimes eightpence, and sometimes tenpence per pound, and we find, too, that he paid ninepence for a powder bag, and one shilling and sixpence for a puff. He used pomatum also, and he tied his hair with ribbons, an adornment with which he had frequently to supply himself, in lengths of two yards at a time, and at a cost of fourpence per yard. This use of ribbon, together with the purchase of a "tailed comb," would seem to show that he wore his hair long behind in a sort of queue. His coats were of various cloths and colours, maroon, drab, blue, and mulberry; his waistcoats are described as of silk and velveret, together with others of the "Burdett" kind, not to speak of virginal white vests, for which he seems to have had a fondness, providing himself on one occasion with no less than three, and at a cost of £1. 5s. 6d. He was apparently particular as to the fineness of his linen, there being an entry relating to the purchase of three pieces of Irish cloth, a material for which in those days you might pay 1s. 9½d. per yard. He buys also cambric for shirt bosoms at the rate of 7s. 3d. per yard, and there is also an item for a small quantity of thick lawn for the same purpose at 8s. per yard. In one entry we find that he "paid Roger Holland for 25 yards of Irish cloth at 1s. 6d. per yard, £1. 17s. 6d.," and in another case he pays "Mrs. Tonge for 2¼ yards cambrick for 6 stocks at 6s. per yard, 13s. 6d." He wore knee breeches, which were of velveret or velveteen, kingscord, or satinet. In this connection garters for the knees and knee buckles are mentioned. Ordinarily he wore thread stockings, which cost him usually 5s. 6d. per pair, but there are also purchases of silk hose, for one pair of which he paid 12s. 9d. To complete his attire he wore shoes which cost him 6s. 6d. per pair, and an entry of 11d. for a pair of buckles would seem to show that they were added for adornment.

Indeed, one interesting feature of a journal of this kind is the opportunity it affords of noting the prices of some commodities which were necessary to John Varey's use or comfort. When we find that he purchased a goose for 3s., and two ducks for 2s., it may be taken as evidence that birds of that kind were cheaper than they are now. So was tobacco, for which 3s. per pound was paid, "Stevenson's" being put down at an extra 6d., that being probably of a better kind. The price of butter is indicated when we find him buying a pound for Sarah Lansdale from Mrs. Tonge for 9d. Sugar is set down at 7d. per pound, and for coffee, of which he sends four pounds into Yorkshire, he pays 1s. 3d. per pound. The cutting and dressing of his hair was sometimes accomplished for 3d., but 6d. is occasionally paid. His breeches knee garters, if of worsted, cost 6d., but something finer was bought for 1s. 1d. His felt hat cost 3s.; "a new hat and girdle," however, was put down at 12s. 6d. He purchases eight yards of satinet, in the rough, at 2s. per yard, of which price they abated him 9d. His gloves cost 2s., and drab cloth is put down at 17s. 6d. per yard.

John Varey, though he was a well-dressed man, yet possessed a frugal mind, and was economical in the purchase of his attire. He seems to have bought many of the materials and then to have given them out to be made up, a lady sometimes performing the work of tailor for him. He buys drab cloth from a Huddersfield man, and stockings from a Kendal man. From a Scotchman he buys marking ink and a set of numbers. At Salford Dirt Fair he buys quite a considerable quantity of cloth and flannel, and there are frequent entries of purchases of fents of velveret, which he sometimes got cut and dyed. These fents with others of satinet were made up into breeches. There are numerous entries for repairing clothes, and the breeches sometimes require re-seating, for which purpose we find in one entry that he has purchased half a yard of velveret. We note, too, that he paid "T. Kent 1s. 6d. for a fent to make three night-caps."

Having got an impression of the outward form of John Varey, with his powdered, be-ribboned hair, his mulberry coat, white waistcoat, satinet breeches, and silk stockings, one is curious to know something about him more immediately personal, but in this direction the entries in his cash-book only provide material for speculation. How old he was, or whether he was a Lancashire man or not the chronicle does not disclose. His parents resided in Yorkshire, apparently at Pontefract, and it may be therefore that our friend was a Yorkshireman.

One of the earliest entries in his book is of a payment of one shilling for the carriage of a box containing a couple of fine shirts and a couple of nightshirts from Pontefract to Manchester. There are several references to journeys into Yorkshire to see the old people, for he appears to have been an affectionate and dutiful son, and on some of these visits he purchases a quantity of liquorice cake, a production for which Pontefract is famous. He has correspondence with home, too, and there are entries of various sums of threepence for postage "paid for a letter from parents." Then there are frequent gifts of tea and tobacco to father and mother. Sometimes the tobacco seems to be given to mother alone, for we come upon "a pound of smoking tobacco for mother," as also "sent per Mr. Harrop for my mother, viz., a pound of tea, 8s.; a pound of tobacco, 3s. 2d." The tea is sometimes Congo, and, on occasion, Green Hyson.

John Varey, though in the service of his Grace the Duke, was not of his household; but in the early part of the chronicle, and for a considerable period, appears as a resident in the house of Sarah Lansdale, to whom he pays for his board and lodging five shillings and sixpence per week, an amount afterwards increased to six shillings and sixpence, but never exceeding that sum. He pays Sarah Lansdale extra for mending his clothes, the amount of this in his quarterly settlement appearing in one instance to be ten shillings and sixpence. There are occasional items also of sixpence to Mary Wood for cleaning his shoes. John Varey's income from his noble master was, as we have seen, never very magnificent, but he was a man of resources, and had other means of earning money. Among these we find that he made out the poor account for the township of Worsley, for which clerkship the overseer paid him sums varying from five to twelve shillings. He also received commissions for the collection of moneys, and had transactions of various kinds, including the purchase and distribution of cheese and potatoes in tolerably large quantities. He was a very thrifty man withal, and in time could lend money, for which interest was paid to him at the rate of five per cent per annum. There are also references to other sources of revenue, and profits from a little partnership arrangement. Like a prudent man, too, he became a member of the Worsley Sick Club, to which he paid the sum of two shillings and twopence quarterly.

His membership of the sick club might possibly have been entered upon in deference to the wishes of his master, inasmuch as we read of His Grace of Bridgewater, that "to those whom he employed he was a good and just master, though a precise and stern one. He looked well after the housing of his colliery workers, and the schooling of their children; establishing shops and markets for them, and taking care that they contributed to a sick club."

Among the items, as set down in his cash-book, is one of half-a-crown due to him from Mr. Gilbert for "crying the rent day," and against this item there is this memorandum, "This J. V. has since received from W. G." Now this is one of those incidental references in the book which open up interesting side avenues that are picturesquely suggestive. This Mr. Gilbert was doubtless the Duke's famous steward, who figures so prominently in those councils of three so often held during the canal-making operations, when the Duke, Brindley, and Gilbert held committee of ways and means as they sat over their pipes and ale in a small public-house on the edge of Chat Moss. This was the Gilbert, too, who, when the Duke was in a dilemma for money, used to ride round among the tenantry of the district raising five pounds here and five pounds there until he had collected enough to pay the week's wages. "On one of these occasions Gilbert was joined by a horseman, and, after some conversation, the meeting ended with an exchange of their respective horses. On alighting afterwards at a lonely inn, which he had not before frequented, Gilbert was surprised to be greeted with evident and mysterious marks of recognition by the landlord, and still more so when the latter expressed a hope that his journey had been successful, and that his saddle-bags were well filled. He was unable to account for the apparent acquaintance of a total stranger with the business and object of his expedition. The mystery was solved by the discovery that he had exchanged horses with a highwayman, who had infested the favoured lanes of Cheshire till his horse had become so well-known that its owner found it convenient to take the first opportunity of providing one less notorious."

But to return to John Varey, though eminently careful and saving, he appears to have taken his pleasure in life. Among his amusements he evidently loved a hand at cards, and in his frank and ingenuous manner he notes down his gains and losses, and the circumstances of the game. Sometimes this is played in Sarah Lansdale's pantry, sometimes in "my parlour," or at John Mosse's, and once we have a record of "won at cards in the servants' hall, 10½d.," which probably relates to the Duke's house. Only once is he tempted to play with dice, and then he loses 1s. 6d. There are records, too, of festive nights at home, as for instance, "Paid expenses at Sarah Lansdale's at a merry night, 6s. 6d.;" or again, "Expenses at S. Lansdale's at a merry night, besides a bottle of rum, 3s., and a quantity of ale, 15s. 2d." On a date a little later than this of the merry night, there is an entry to the effect that he "Paid James Massey for a sett of strings and a bridge, and repairing a violin which I borrowed of Mr. Tonge, 2s. 6d." Possibly the violin had been brought into active service at the aforesaid merry-making. Occasionally, like other men he requires medicine, and so we come upon entries relating to the purchase of Scotch pills at 6d. per box, and of Turkey rhubarb at 2s. 6d. per oz.

It should not be supposed, however, that John Varey was a man inordinately fond of amusements, or one who indulged in any excesses. The impression that one gets from his honest cash account is quite other than that. He was apparently a man of a very well regulated life, generous and charitable within the limits of his slender means. Such little pleasures as have been noted among his accounts are spread over a wide period, and there are equally clear evidences of his good-natured unselfishness. People came to him for small loans, and he gave little sums in relief to widows and people who happened accidents, colliers, and others. We find, too, that he lent John Aston, a miner, £1. 1s., which was duly repaid. Again, he gives to Nancy Butterworth a bottle of wine, and at Mrs. Osbaldeston's he pays for a bottle of red wine for Charles Rainsford, 2s. To Robert Crippin, who has lost a son, he gives 6d. His gifts to his parents have been already noted, and once when on a visit to Yorkshire we find that he "gave to mother to buy sundries £2. 2s." Among his gifts are two calico gowns to his sisters, and it is worthy of note that the cost of such material was then 2s. 4d. per yard.

In going through John Varey's accounts we find many references to his little journeyings on His Grace's business or his own, but his movements are mainly of a local kind, never extending further than Liverpool, save when he pays his visits to Yorkshire. Sometimes he is on horseback, and we find among his purchases a hand whip which costs 6s., and a pair of steel spurs, 2s. 6d. Sometimes he uses the coach, but very frequently we find him travelling by canal to Runcorn or Manchester, and he appears to be on friendly terms with one Captain Dobson, who is remembered by a New Year's gift of two shillings. The passage to Manchester cost sixpence, from Throstlenest to Worsley, fourpence, and the "Boat to and from Runcorn" is set down at four shillings and sixpence.

Through many pages of his book John Varey deals with his own affairs as a bachelor dwelling in the house of good Sarah Lansdale, but there came a time when he had to settle up finally with that lady. The record tells that the payment is "Jany. 17th, 1784, the time I left and was married." But previous to that date we find that on New Year's Day he has "Paid Mr. Olivant for a gold ring 7s. 10d.," and also "For a pair of silver buckles 19s.," to which latter entry is added the words, "gave them my Dr wife." Then between that date and the wedding he gets his hair cut and dressed, gives Captain Dobson his New Year's gift, receives his year's salary of £60 from His Grace of Bridgewater, and has a merry night at Thorpe's, which cost him two shillings and sixpence. On the

18th of January we find these entries :—

> Paid for licence to marry Martha Tonge (this day was married), £1. 11s. 6d.
> Expences at Eccles and Worsley when married, 14s. 6d.
> Ringers, 5s.
> Expences with Will Greenwood, 1s. 6d.

Subsequently there are payments "for a barrel of ale" had at our wedding, for rum, wedding gloves, and other incidentals of the marriage feast. Matty has five guineas given to her to "buy sundries," and then little more than two months after comes the entry of "wine and physic for Matty when sick," which is ominous, and early in June following we find "Parson's dues, hearse, and expenses to Middleton, £1. 7s. 6d.; coffin, £1. 7s. 9d." And still later, "Paid Miles Taylor for cutting the inscription on my wife's gravestone, 5s. 3d." After this sad event there is an increasing seriousness about John Varey. He buys "Hervey's Meditations," and many other books of a meditative kind. On April 3, 1785, we read that he "Spent at Manchester, on hearing Mr. Wesley preach there, 1s. 4d." On referring to John Wesley's journal, we find that being on his way to Ireland, he preached at Manchester on the date in question, which was Sunday. Among John Varey's purchases of devotional books, we find that he paid Mr. Pawson, "a travelling Methodist preacher from Manchester," one shilling for a new edition of "J. Watts on Future State," and how he subscribed to the publication of the Rev. Mr. Fawell's octavo, entitled, "The Principles of Sound Policy Enforced." He pays his subscriptions as duly to the Sunday School as to his sick club; he subscribes also to "A scheme for raising money to build a house;" he drinks his glass of rum, reads his newspaper and his devotional books, and in later days shows clearly that he has given serious thought to theological controversy, and has come under the influence of the Swedenborgian views, which were then quite new in England.

After recording an amount of two shillings "Spent at Flixton feast," we come upon this, "Spent at Manchester, seeing the Rev. Mr. Clowes, one shilling." It will be remembered that the Rev. John Clowes, Rector of St. John's Church, Manchester, was the introducer of Swedenborgianism to this country, and also a voluminous writer on that new doctrine, regarding which John Varey may have gone for enlightenment. This apostle of Swedenborg was just then exercising a great influence over the people, not only of his own church, but the inhabitants of surrounding villages. It is said of him by his biographer that "He used to ride in the morning to some manufacturing village . . . and as soon as his arrival was known at the factory where most of the members worked, the bell was rung; the people left work and collected in a large room allowed for the purpose by the proprietors." It may have been in some such way that John Varey first became attracted to the preacher, and so was led to visit him, an incident which reminds one how sixteen years later the youth, De Quincey, also visited that quiet Rectory of St. John's, and of the impression the Opium Eater has left us of its occupant. Among the last entries in John Varey's cash-book is one relating to the expenditure of "Eightpence for breakfast at J. Osbaldeston's, with the Rev. J. Clowes," and there in that worshipful company one may fittingly take leave of him.

NOTE.—John Varey's Cash-Book is now in the Manchester Free Reference Library, to which it has been presented by Mr. Roeder.

A NOTE ON NOTTINGHAM.

"AND I will unto fair Nottingham go," says Robin Hood in one of those old ballads wherein the town figures so frequently as the scene of the bold outlaw's exploits, and is so often praised for the fairness of its aspect. "The Queen of the Midlands, picturesquely enthroned on the northern bank of the silvery and meandering river Trent," are words the modern guide book writer uses as he starts out on his journey descriptive of the many attractions of the Nottingham of to-day. The town has changed vastly since the time when

> Robin Hood walked the forest free,
> Under the fresh green leaf;
> And the proud sheriff of Nottingham,
> He knew it to his grief.

By virtue of a newly acquired dignity, it is now known as a city, but though it has increased in bulk and thereby "bulged beyond the lines of beauty" in some particulars, the local topographer is still justified in regarding it as one of the fairest and most picturesque of our manufacturing centres.

Prefaced to the old ballad already referred to is a quaint little picture of Nottingham castle, which shows you a towered pile of masonry, suggestive of ruinous conditions perched upon a high rock, on the face of which is a notice board indicating the way "To the Baths." At the foot of the rock and in the roadway, a four-horsed mail coach is standing with passengers on the outside seated about the driver, who holds the reins and the whip, while the guard in the rear is blowing a lengthened horn. Travelling to Nottingham from Cottonopolis in these days and journeying thither, not in a mail coach but by the Midland railway, as you approach the city, looking leftward from your carriage window, your eye falls upon what is still known as Nottingham castle, but instead of the towered and embattled walls of a feudal stronghold the bold precipitous rock is crested with a pile of modern balustraded masonry, dignified in appearance and of a classic style of architecture. When you have reached the city, though you may be interested in many things discoverable there, you cannot do better than make your way in the first instance to its uplifted castle rock, for there you will find as it were the key of your situation. As you pass through the intermediate streets, you are made aware in their varying gradients that Nottingham is built in great part upon rising ground, of which the castle rock is the predominating height. Round this rock the city has grouped itself and grown, and for the stronghold it maintained—as for a coveted habitation—kings and nobles have contested, the record of its varied fortunes in this regard furnishing much that is picturesque and romantic, as you will find if you consult the pages of the local historians. Standing at the base of this rock, clothed here and there with trees and shrubs, and furnishing nesting places in its crevices and crannies for numerous doves seen flying in and out there, you note that it is of a sandstone nature, and that it is marked with cave-like openings and recesses suggestive of subterranean passages and hiding places. This feature of it is interesting, because if you enquire further, you will find that the early inhabitants of Nottingham were, in a sense, cave men, who seem to have burrowed in the prevailing sandstone rock to furnish themselves with dwelling places. In outlying parts of the city you may still see these cavernous excavations, and will learn that rock-cellars of considerable depth and size exist beneath the present buildings of the interior.

Ascending to the rock summit by the Lenton Road, and passing through a gateway, you find yourself within the spacious castle enclosure, with a fair broad space of green turf on one side, and on the other, occupying the highest point, the terraced stone building, still spoken of as the castle, with its outward parapets resting on the extreme verge of the precipitous crag. On these terraces you will see openings which disclose the existence and entrance to that subterranean passage, known as "Mortimer's Hole," the square lighting spaces of which were visible to you on the rock face from below, and which proved so useful to the adventurous party, who, on a memorable night in the year 1330, gained access to the castle by means of it and secretly effected the capture of Roger Mortimer, Earl of March. When you have entered the wide portals of the modern castle, you find yourself not in a feudal stronghold but in a temple dedicated to the arts, and representative of that high culture which is the crowning grace of the industrial life of which it is the latest expression. As you wander through this Palace of Art—otherwise known as a Museum—with its broad staircases, spacious corridors and noble rooms, you will find the lengthened wall spaces of some of the apartments covered with pictures, recognisable among these reflections of the city's history being portraits of local celebrities whom Nottingham has delighted to honour, while in others you come upon rich displays of products illustrative of the arts and crafts, decorative and industrial.

From the terrace walks, looking over the parapet there, you get fine prospects, reaching far beyond the smoke-dimmed area to distant green and wooded un-

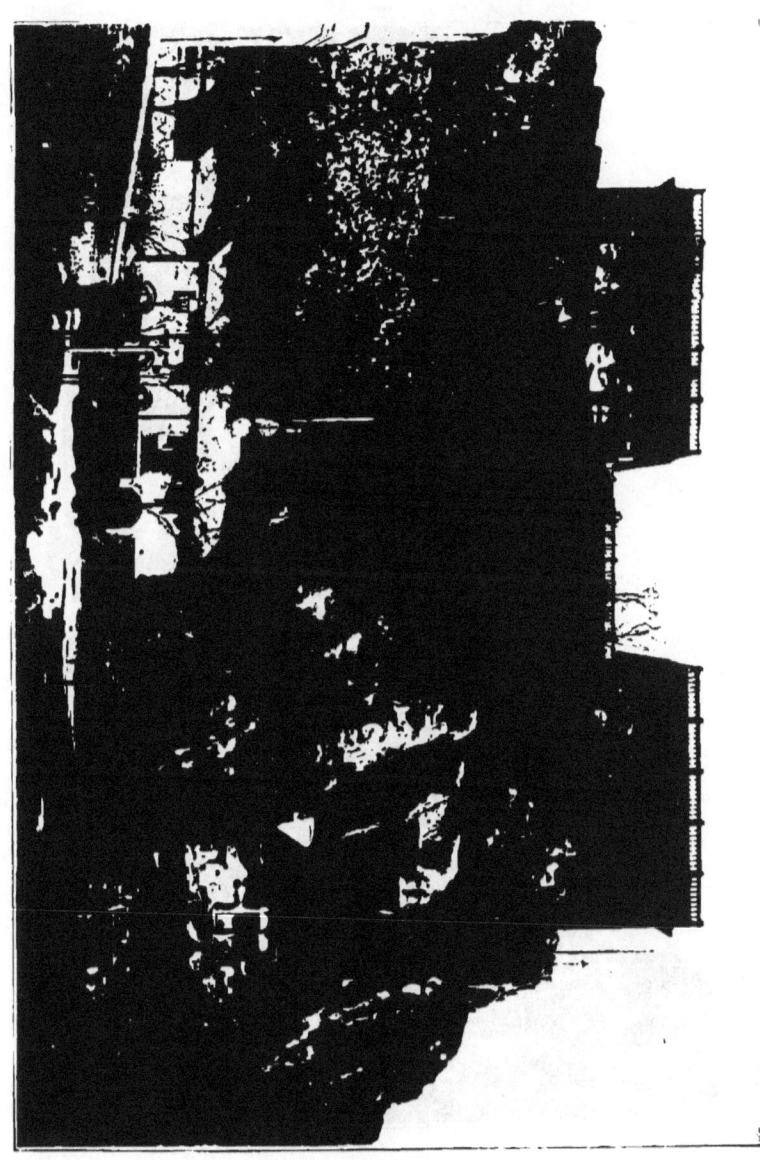

NOTTINGHAM CASTLE.

MARKET PLACE, NOTTINGHAM

dulations, with the vale of Trent lying between and the river—"the silvery Trent" as they like to call it here—flowing by in the near distance, notable for the handsome "Trent bridge," which, with its broad-spanned graceful arches, gives access from the south. The city itself stretches out widely beneath you, for it has a population estimated at a quarter of a million, and so you look out over a great acreage of roofs, from which rise spires and towers, and tall chimneys also, the evidences of its busy manufacturing industries. It is not a hard featured place, for from your eyrie of observation you can look down upon bowery nooks with red-tiled roofs, of houses islanded amid "the nestling green." Near by you have a spacious boulevard and park-like enclosures suggestive of other open spaces existing elsewhere, popular places of resort, such as the Arboretum and that extensive tract of eighty acres known as "The Forest," reminding you in its name, as does also "Robin Hood's Chase," of the time when the merry greenwood reached to the edge of the town. Among the heraldic symbols which go to make up the arms of the city there is reference to this association with the forest, and on the corporation seal there is shown a Norman castle with four circular towers enclosed within a circular wall.

If you are of an enquiring disposition and are curious to know how Nottingham has grown to its present dimensions, from conditions in which its feudal stronghold was the predominating influence, you will have, among other things, to study the history of machine-made lace in England, for it is to this light and delicate form of manufacture that the Nottingham folk have mainly devoted themselves. It is a long story, but you will find it most interestingly told in a compendious volume by the late Mr. William Felkin, and you will be distinctly helped to a mechanical knowledge of the lace industry if you have an opportunity of inspecting one of those numerous factories whose mill chimneys are in evidence beneath you.

From these sources you will learn how lace-making in the machine form is a development from framework knitting, and so it has come about that the hosiery and lace-making industries have grown up side by side. Regarding this evolution of lace-making it may be admissible to repeat what one has elsewhere set down briefly. Lace-work, as you know, consists of reticulated work—that is it has crossed lines so arranged as to form open spaces capable of infinite variety, from the plainest loop or mesh to the most complicated and elaborate interlacement of threads in artistic ornamentation. Some definitions of this network are curious, one of them being that it is something "with holes in it tied together by a string." Dr. Johnson's definition is that network is "anything reticulated or decussated at equal distances with interstices between the intersections." All lace then is in

LONG ROW, NOTTINGHAM

some form or other network, though all network is not necessarily lace in the ordinary acceptation of the term. A fishing-net would hardly be regarded as a piece of lace-work, yet the first worker of such a net was a pioneer in lace-making. In this connection it is worthy of note as a curious fact, that one of the inventors of lace machinery, Robert Brown, of New Radford, Nottinghamshire, took out in 1802 a patent for his invention of "a machine for the purpose of manufacturing, by this more speedy, simple and neat method, fishing-nets, horse-nets, garden-nets, furniture-nets, nets for wearing apparel, and all other articles of network, having the same common diamond mesh and knot hitherto tied by the hand, with the netting needle in fishing-nets." Then again, we should not be disposed to regard a knitted stocking as in any sense a piece of lace-work, but it is nevertheless a fact that in stocking-knitting machine-made lace had its origin. The old lace-making by hand may be described broadly as falling into two great divisions— needle-point and pillow lace. Needle-point, with its cut lace forms grew out of embroidery; pillow lace, a later art, was constructed from threads drawn from bobbins hung round a pillow and crossed, according to the will of the worker, over pins stuck in front of the cushion. What is called bobbin net in the machine form is the outcome of this pillow-made lace.

To what beautiful intricacies of design the hand workers attained, with their interlacements of thread in point and pillow lace is well known, but though the machines which afterwards took the place of human fingers were able to imitate these designs with more or less truthfulness, it was from the stocking knitter rather than from the hand-lace worker, that the idea of the first lace-making machine was gained. Knitting by means of needles consists in making and controlling the arrangement of a series of loops from a thread, but these loops are drawn pretty closely together and do not assume the form of the open mesh-work. As is pretty well known, the first stocking-frame was made at the close of the sixteenth century, by the Rev. William Lee, M.A., of St. John's College, Cambridge, and the origin of his invention has been associated with more or less of doubtful, picturesque and romantic incident.

From experiments on this stocking-frame made somewhere about 1764, it was found possible to govern the movements of the needles and thread so as to produce the interstices between the loops and so form a *looped* net. Afterwards machines were constructed by which a net was made of *twisted* meshes, like that of the hand-made pillow lace. The history of the inventions which succeeded these earlier efforts is a strange, eventful one, full of stirring, and in many cases, tragic interest. Ingenious men laboured and toiled under adverse conditions and with varied results to accom-

plish these interlacements of threads by mechanical means. Some achieved fortune and fame, but many of them broke their hearts in the effort, and ended their days in poverty and neglect, while others went mad or committed suicide. Little by little, by the selection of the fittest, by adaptation and combination the lace-making machines as we see them to-day were constructed. In the early manufacture of hosiery and lace, yarns of various kinds—silk, worsted and flax—were used. At a later date cotton was introduced, and the circumstances of its adoption are associated with an interesting and familiar chapter in the history of cotton spinning. To the early inventors of cotton spinning machinery, Nottingham was a place of adoption or refuge from persecution. Here came Hargreaves with his spinning jenny, flying from the Blackburn mob who had broken into his house and destroyed his new-fangled machine. Here, along with a partner, he built a mill, one of the earliest of its kind in England. Here, too, from fear of receiving the same treatment, came Arkwright with his spinning rollers, taking out for them his first patent and setting them to work in a mill driven by horse power. But cotton spinning was not to find here its home though the yarns which were the product of it were destined to occupy a larger place in lace-making than all others, and so it has come about that to Lancashire the Nottingham manufacturer still must go for the materials of which his lace thread is made.

Passing out from the castle gate you find yourself on the threshold of mercantile and manufacturing Nottingham, for if you take your way along Houndsgate you will notice there on the signboards of warehouses some prominent names associated with local industries, and when you emerge from this main thoroughfare upon the wider space where stands the church of St. Peter, and from that point proceed forth along the Pavements Low and High, and so to the ancient parish church of St. Mary, you will find yourself in the region known as "The Lace Market." Here, among the warehouses devoted to the handling and distribution of light lace tissues, in the absence of that heavier street traffic to which one is accustomed in Cottonopolis, business seems, by contrast, to be carried on amid quieter surroundings, and with an atmosphere about it of a more reposeful calm. The same effect is produced upon you when you find yourself in some green-embowered court occupied by professors of law and accountancy. Busy enough, however, Nottingham is, especially on market days, and in the neighbourhood of that great market place, which is one of its distinguishing features. Here you have a great triangular space, said to be the largest open market place in the country, and occupying an area of nearly five acres and a half. At the base of this triangle you have an old-fashioned stuccoed building, known as the Exchange, with a statue of Justice appropriately surmounting it. On the other sides you have lengthened lines of lofty irregular buildings, the basements of which are mainly occupied as shops, many of them with piazzas or covered ways in front. Notably among these buildings is that line of them known as the "Long Row." These shops of the market place, like others in the streets that lead up to it, have a bright business-like look—many of them are spacious and handsome. The open market space is occupied with a great array of stalls devoted to the sale of multitudinous wares. On roadway and footway you find yourself among a busy throng of people, and as you pass up and down among them you have a sense of being in a centre of brisk activity. This market place, of which the Nottingham folk are very proud, has at times been used for other purposes than buying or selling. Here in the old election days the "lambs" have disported themselves, and in times of popular disturbance it has served as a convenient rallying place. Once a year it is converted into a vast pleasure ground and becomes the scene of the famous "Goose Fair," which formerly lasted twenty-one days and has now diminished to three. This fair is held in October, and is described in the local guide book as "Nottingham's carnival." Like other institutions of the kind it has felt the influence of Time's changeful hand, but, as a scene for holiday making, there is still a disinclination to let Goose Fair go. Of the crowds that have flocked to it in the old days one gleans an amusing illustration from a local historian, who tells us that "During the time that Marshal Tallard was a prisoner at Nottingham, it is said he wrote to the King of France, telling him to continue the war for England was nearly drained of men. Shortly afterwards he went to see Goose Fair, and he immediately wrote off to France counselling his majesty to give up the war, because he had seen as many men in one English market place as could conquer the whole of France!"

As the purpose of this slight sketch of Nottingham is not of the guide book kind, but only the recording of general impressions in outline, it remains but to say that as the visitor makes his progress through the city by cars that traverse the tram-railed streets, or on foot along quieter byways, he will find much to interest him expressive of its many-sided life. Its old churches appeal to his archæological taste, and in its more modern Guildhall, University College, Free Library, Post Office, and other public and private buildings, he will recognise how in stone and terra-cotta, with features of Gothic, Flemish and other styles, its architectural attractions are growing and developing. In your wanderings, too, you cannot fail to come upon some of the numerous old almshouses which were provided for the benefit of poor folk by aforetime benefactors, among whom you may recognise one with the quaintly flavoured name of Barnaby Wartnaby. Prominent among these almshouses is Collins' Hospital, railed off from the busy street within a green, tree-dotted enclosure. Alongside similar green spaces, and in side avenues, you may on market days meet with some other survivals of the earlier time, in the form of old-fashioned travel-stained carriers' wagons, with hooded covers and with names on them of villages near or remote, pleasantly suggestive to you of things pastoral, and of that country green—lying round about—whose fair landscape features were revealed to you in your outlook from the castle rock.

RYE AND WINCHELSEA.

———◆———

EARLY on a beautiful autumn morning—to adopt the manner of certain old-fashioned novelists—a solitary pedestrian might have been seen making his way up the steep slope to the High Street of the quaint old town of Rye, on the Sussex coast. So early was it that the streets were silent and deserted, and as he walked along he woke up the sleeping dogs that lay in the sunshine. A lonely policeman standing in watchful contemplation at a point where he could command several avenues of approach, eyed him curiously as he passed by, doubtless speculating on the purpose of his pilgrimage. If that guardian of the peace had questioned him, the traveller would have had to confess that he was pursuing a sentimental journey, the nature of which he might have found some difficulty in explaining to a prosaic mind. He had passed through the hop gardens and orchards of Kent staying here and there, but always he had in his mind as he travelled a vision of two old decayed seaports which formed, as it were, the ultimate end of his journey. These were Rye and Winchelsea, and it was to Rye that he had come first.

Rye stands picturesquely upon a steep hill overlooking Romney Marsh and all the flat land that lies between it and the sea. It is a pet place for painters, and you will doubtless have seen many views of it on the walls of picture exhibitions. With its quaint red-roofed houses, crowned by a grand old church with broad square tower and squat peaked roof; its Ypres tower and Landgate, all clustered in most picturesque grouping on the steep ground that rises so abruptly from the flat marsh land through which the river winds seaward, with ships lying idly in their haven under the hill; all these things present many points of interest in form and colour to the artist eye. Though he did not lay claim to the possession of such an eye, these varied features of interest were not lost upon the stranger as he saw them in the brightness of the early morning, and canopied by a sky of brilliant blue. Neither was the visitor insensible to the charm of antiquity that clings to the place, to the interest that belongs to it as one of the Cinque ports, to its stories of sea fights, and of incursions of the French who more than once devastated it with fire and sword, not sparing its ancient church in their ravages. This charm of antiquity and picturesque beauty led him to turn his steps in the first instance to the church, where he looked up to the great tower and saw the gilded clock with the antique figures in the front of it that strike the quarters on the bells, said to be of Elizabethan date, and the oldest going clock of its kind in the country. Then he crossed the churchyard by the path among the graves, and so to the Ypres tower built by William de Ypres in the twelfth century, and then down by the steep stairway to the river and the boats, and so up again by another stairway to the Landgate. Then he walked aimlessly about the streets noting the architecture of the houses, coming unexpectedly upon odds and ends of ancientry, among which was an edifice that showed some signs of beauty, left after much rough usage, and which once sheltered a community of Austin Friars, but is now used as a storehouse for merchandise, for here in this port of Rye they deal in wool, corn, timber, hops, and oak bark, and among their industries they include that of shipbuilding.

But, added to all the charms of ancient beauty and picturesqueness, there was one which was predominant in the mind of the pilgrim, the admission of which might be accounted a weakness. The spell of a novelist's fiction was upon the scene, and it was this that had mainly drawn him hither. Thackeray had written a story called *Denis Duval*, which he never

RYE.

MERMAID STREET, RYE.

lived to finish, and the opening chapters of it were associated with this old town of Rye and that other one of Winchelsea hard by. That is a strange power of the writer of fiction to be able to associate his legends with scenes and places so that they are ever afterwards inseparable. Dropping the third person, I may say that Thackeray for me possesses this power in an eminent degree, and I may as well confess that his story, fictitious though it might be, was as real to me in Rye as the more authentic history of the place. "And what for no?" as a Scotchman would say. Are we not all the victims of the people of vivid imagination? Have I not sat on the coach that carried me through the Trosachs and the scenery of the *Lady of the Lake* and listened to an enthusiastic native of that land as he recited lines from Scott's poems, and pointed out the places of stirring incident therein described, with all the earnestness of one who no more doubted the fact of the fight between Fitz-James and Roderick Dhu than he did of the existence to this day of Coilantogle Ford where that mighty combat took place?

And so it was of Thackeray and Denis Duval that I was thinking as I walked through the silent grass-grown streets of Rye. Perhaps the fascination arose in a great measure from the fact that these scenes were among the last that filled the novelist's mind, and formed the background of his unfinished story.

As I walked about it seemed to me as if the lad Denis had really lived there, had gone to Pocock's grammar school, and lodged with Mr. Rudge the grocer in one of those old-fashioned shops in the main street, to have like me wandered about the churchyard on the hill with the pollarded trees round about it, and the shining houses showing between, and have seen, on some such sunny morning, the grey old tower and the orange-stained roof showing against the blue of the sky, with the starlings and noisy jackdaws flying about them. Sundays, as he tells us, he liked best at Rye, or rather every other Sunday, because then, he says, "I went away quite early and walked three miles to mother and grandfather at Winchelsea."

When I had rambled about Rye, I walked those three miles to Winchelsea, which stands on a wooded hill overlooking the marshes. Taking that direction I dropped down the steep streets of Rye, to where the ships were lying in the docks, and then passed out to the smooth flat road that traverses the level marsh which lies between the two hills. Walking along this road, between the dikes with the long feathery grasses growing in them, you get a sight, looking seawards, of a ruined castle lying four-square and desolate on the marshy track. This is Camber Castle, and beyond it on the coast you can see a line of Martello towers. When you are on the edge of that tree-clad slope, where Winchelsea stands, with the decayed town

behind, you see these marsh lands stretching away to the sea, with the grey old castle standing lonely on the flat tract between. Denis Duval used to say that often there came to him a vision of a road leading down through the old gate to the blue marshes and shining towers and gables of Rye on the slope not far away.

I went up to Winchelsea through that old gate, and saw what is left of the town, which has been shrinking through the centuries, until where once were streets are now green fields, and on the rest lies the sleepy quiet of a village rather than a town. Winchelsea has had a strange eventful history. The site of it originally was away down on the low-lying land, but more than once the sea came upon it with destructive purposes and eventually overwhelmed it. Before that time it had been a nest of pirates and sea rovers, whom Edward the First, then a prince, had found it necessary to bring to a sense of law and order, to that end storming the place and taking possession of it. After the sea had destroyed it, the piratical folk petitioned this same king to rebuild the town for them, which he did, granting them land on the tree-tufted slope where it now stands. The flat top of this Higham Hill was laid out in squares with streets at right angles in a most orderly fashion, as you may see yet. More than once after this have the French come down upon the town and plundered it, as also did the Spaniards.

Fighting, smuggling, and piracy are mixed up with the history of the old port, from which the sea itself seems to have receded, the harbour having become choked. In better days the inhabitants burrowed into the hill on which it is built, and made crypts and caves that extended for great distances, where they stored wines, and doubtless also smuggled goods. If you have read the novel you will remember that Denis Duval was born here, and lived with his grandfather, the perruquier, who had a share in a smuggler's craft, and that he tells us that many of their neighbours also had ventures of that kind. I breakfasted in the little inn which overlooks the broad green space with the fine old church with ruined arches and columns still clinging to it, the ash tree were John Wesley preached, and the quaint old Town Hall. Later I walked about the sleepy streets lying straggling among fields and gardens, and had talk with stray people I met about the crypts and subterranean spaces extending beneath the town and out in the fields, and then to the windmill on the green knoll close by. I saw the Friary, an old house embowered in trees which was surely the Priory where the Westons lived, and the scene of some interesting episodes in Thackeray's story, and then I passed out under an old town gate which lies away in the fields, and so among hop gardens and the green country found my way back to my inn at Hastings.

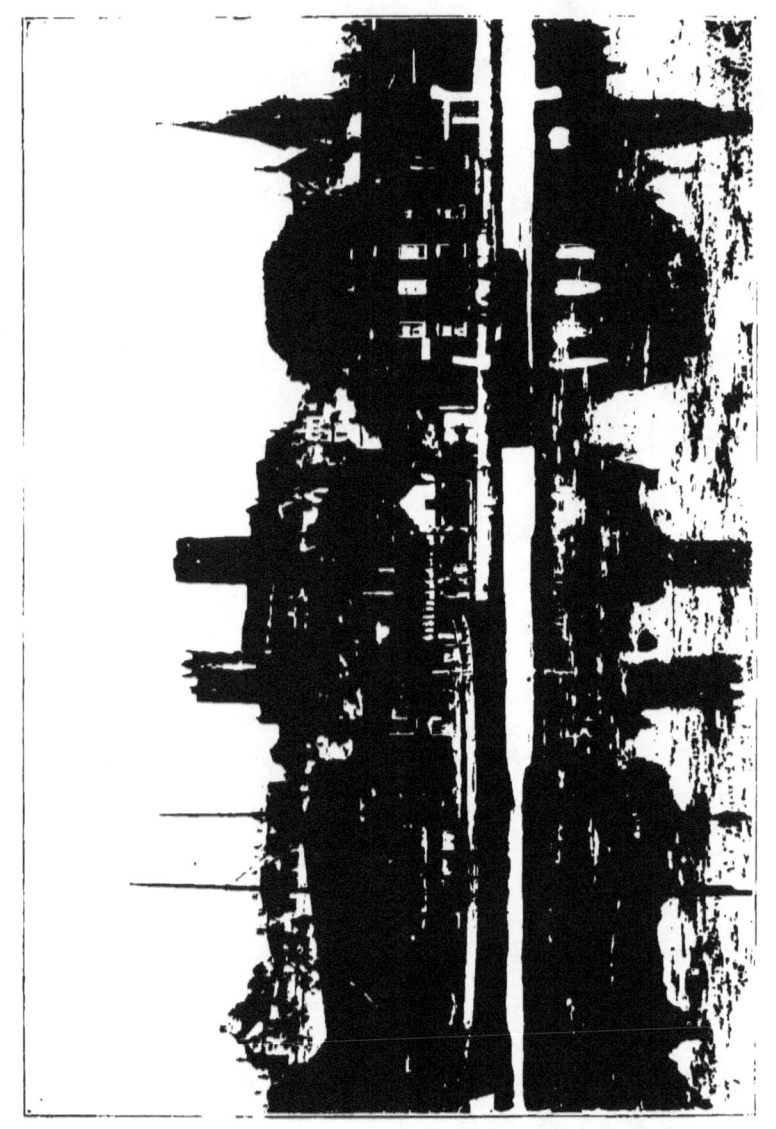

LINCOLN

YARMOUTH TO BARMOUTH.

YARMOUTH in the east and Barmouth in the west marked the extreme limits of travel, and a crow flying between would take nearly a straight line; but only in a restricted sense was it proposed to follow the direction of the bird. Yarmouth itself was to be approached in easy and varied stages, beginning at Lincoln, and there was to be much zigzagging about in the fens and elsewhere before at Stamford something like a straightforward course was entered upon.

The autumn of the year, now a remote one, in which this journey was taken, was remarkable for its drenching, devastating rains in harvest time. In the midst of this rainy season there came a day of charming beauty, bright but delusive, and it was upon this September day that I started out, along with a friend who was to accompany me throughout the journey. Taking train by that line of railway which is now known as the Great Central, we were carried through a hill country which travellers of the olden time regarded as romantic, the wild gorges of the outlying barriers of the Peak being visible as we passed the hollow, beneath the moorland, in which Glossop lies. Then beyond this through the great watershed of the Longdendale Valley—where Cottonopolis has great storages of water—a land of streams and tufted heather and gritstone crag, and so through the great tunnel at Woodhead, and over the ridge and by Penistone to Sheffield. There we found the railway platform crowded with anglers armed with fishing-rods, landing-nets, and baskets, all, like ourselves, bound for the fens. A thousand or more, we were told, had just been sent on, and these were waiting for another train. It was the occasion of one of their great fishing excursions, and for the next few days these anglers were to be found scattered over the dykes and watercourses between Lincoln and Boston. In no other town in the kingdom has Izaak Walton so many disciples as in this of Sheffield. Beyond the smoke of Sheffield we emerged into a country which became less wooded and gradually widened itself out into wavy slopes, with harvest fields dotted with farmsteads, and then flattened itself out into low meadows with dykes and slow streams, fringed with poplars and pollarded willows.

STONEBOW, LINCOLN.

At Retford we were already among windmills and at the threshold of the slow-moving fen country. Redeford, as it was anciently called, suggests reeds in the river, the very name of which is Idle. At Torksey we crossed the brimming Trent, getting as we passed a glimpse of a ruined castle of mellow brickwork, with shattered walls and window spaces relieved against a soft blue afternoon sky, and of a broad-sailed barge coming slowly along down the wan water, which flowed lip-full between low grassy banks and pastures with cattle feeding in them. Then we passed on, parallel to the great Foss Dyke, until we reached Lincoln, where we took up our abode at an old-fashioned inn in the main street, close by an ancient gateway known as the Stone Bow. Lincoln is a city set upon a hill in the midst of a wide plain, and the cathedral crowns it like a diadem. It is crammed full of antiquities. Romans, Danes, Saxons, and Normans have left their mark upon it; and in the matter of ancient edifices it has been said that the very pigstyes have been constructed with the wrecks of them. It had over fifty-two churches, besides the cathedral, but has now only a dozen, it may be. Going up the main street from the station, you cross the Witham, and get sight of old wharves, projecting gables, masts, and shipping. Then you come to the ancient gateway, the Stone Bow, spanning the street, with statues in the niches and an old guildhall over the arch. Beyond this, climbing the street between the old gabled houses and shops, you come to the Steep which brings you to the crest of the hill, where the cathedral stands with the Conqueror's Norman castle close by, and many ancient houses and buildings, notably a Jew's house with a carved front of great antiquity. Hereabouts, in old days, the traders were to be found, one thoroughfare being known as the "Drapery." On this steep slope of the hill there are many pleasant houses and gardens fringing the cathedral close. If you go beyond the cathedral and castle you can leave the city by passing under a veritable Roman archway, known as the Westport.

When we had rested at our inn we climbed the Steep to look at the cathedral, and out upon the dyke-bordered fens visible in the twilight beyond the red-tiled roofs, the scattered churches, the orchards, and garden enclosures. It was pleasant to loiter about the close until the great tower of the cathedral—with its highest window traceries showing lines of richly carved crockettings—could be seen relieved against a pearly, star-lit sky; to hear through the silence the tolling of the curfew bell, and, when it had ceased, to see the solitary ringer emerge from the tower and flit across the close to disappear in one of those quiet houses within the precincts. Such incidents as these may seem trivial and unimportant, but they linger in the memory. It was pleasant, too, on the Sunday that followed to take a more leisurely survey of the cathedral, to marvel at the vastness of its proportions, the beauty of its west front, its Galilee porch, and its fine east window; to mark the gradations of style, from the early Norman arches of severest simplicity, the remains of the church which Remigius built soon after the Conquest, to the most elaborate decorated Gothic; but to marvel most of all at the wondrous carving in evidence wherever the eye might turn, in doorway, pillar, arcaded wall-space, string course, or window place; then afterwards to sit, during service, near the altar and the tomb of the pious founder and look down the angel choir, with the sunlight shining through the painted windows and casting a glory of reflected colour on arch and pillar.

Coming out into the sunlit close what could be more enjoyable than to lounge about the peaceful enclosure, for the close of Lincoln cathedral has beauties of its own with its old stone gateways overgrown with mosses and long grasses; its vine-clad, steep-roofed houses, and its palace and gardens, though the general effect just then was marred by the work of restoration going on at the west end. Among the litter and débris there was a heap of broken plaster which the workmen had cast aside. Examining it, we found that interwoven with it and binding it together were long feathery-tufted grasses as complete as when taken from the fens, where they grew one knows not how many centuries ago. Near to the cathedral close is the Castle, approached through a square which has an ancient arched gateway at the end of it, through which you may pass into the walled enclosure and see a modern prison and courts of justice, and also be free to climb a lofty tower and get another outlook over the fen and other wide lands lying round about you. On a more recent visit than this which is being described one saw the outer square under picturesque conditions. The footways and windows of the old houses were crowded with spectators, and in the open space was a platform covered with crimson cloth, and occupied by the mayor, the city fathers, and other corporation dignitaries. The occasion was the visit of a Lincolnshire regiment of the line which was marching through, and which it was arranged should halt here to receive, through its commanding officer, an address of congratulation. In due season the soldiers filed into the square between the crowds, whose cheering at the sight of the tattered regimental colours rose above the martial music. With interchange of complimentary speeches the colonel received his address of welcome, and then, the ceremony ended, the soldiers marched away again to their music through the cathedral close.

On the morrow we took train to Boston, going by the Witham side, and getting our first true impression of the landscape of the fen country. What it was in its untamed state of wild marshes, haunted by waterfowl, before it was drained and tilled, can only be imagined; but, as Charles Kingsley says, it still retains a beauty of its own, the great fen country, a beauty as of the sea, of boundless expanse and freedom. It is not monotonous, though there are straight lines everywhere, in dyke and stream, and deep-rutted roads raised above the level of the sheep-dotted pastures and fields of grain. The great expanse is relieved with hamlets and villages, often clustering about fine old churches, with broad-sailed windmills, farmsteads and granges peeping from clumps of thickly-foliaged trees. It is not without beauty of colour, too, this lush green fen land. Even under a grey aqueous sky, which canopied it to the distant horizon, there was over all a prevailing soft sweetness of tone, lighted up with patches of colour from red-tiled roofs or some gaily-painted barge lying moored among the long sedges that grow in the lazy streams. About these watercourses that flow through the rich black loamy soil, fringed with long waving fen grasses, there is a beauty of—

> Creeping mosses and clambering weeds,
> And willow branches hoar and dank,
> And wavy swell of soughing reeds,
> And silvery marish flowers that throng
> The desolate creeks and pools among.

This fen land has a background of picturesque history, and has been roamed over and fought for by Norsemen, Danes, Romans, Anglo-Saxons, and Normans. It has also been fought with by more peaceful combatants, by whose unremitting labours the wildness of it has been subdued, so that the vast plain has become a fruitful garden, and the wilderness has been made to blossom as the rose.

Boston is associated in one's memory with red-tiled houses; a wide, irregular, open market place; a tidal river, with brown-sailed vessels lying by a quay, with a fragrance of seeds and pinewood about it; but chiefly with the church of St. Botolph, whose great, square, pinnacled tower, built up in balconied stories, pierced by windows, and surmounted by an open lantern on the model of the cathedral at Antwerp, rises from the muddy bank of the river, and in its gigantic height dwarfs all the town beneath. Mariners at sea and dwellers in the fens far away recognise it as a landmark, and speak of it familiarly as Boston Stump. We climbed a great way up the tower, and looked down upon the town below, the fens beyond, and then out to the salt marshes and the dull sea water of Boston deeps. Out of the town we wandered, passing through a public garden of loveliest vegetation and richest colour of flowers, along the willow-fringed stream, past windmills and quaint, yellow-washed, water-side houses, until we came to where the river winds out to the dim distance between high banks and a wide seagull-haunted sedgy waste, the course of it marked by tall posts, where lights are

BOSTON CHURCH.

BARGATE GREEN AND CHURCH, BOSTON.

KING'S LYNN.

MARKET PLACE, EAST DEREHAM

hung to guide the mariner in his night voyaging. Our walk ended at the ancient church of Skirbeck, which overlooks the river, and is dedicated to St. Nicholas, the patron saint of fishermen, whose graves within its ancient enclosure are marked by many curious epitaphs. Returning to Boston we rambled about its streets, and rested for awhile at an inn, and listened to the chimes of St. Botolph's tinkling out a tune high up in air—an imitation, we were told, of those at Antwerp. A horsey man with whom we had some talk, spoke derisively of that aërial music, and complained of the money that had been wasted upon it. This horsey person disclosed a curious disposition on the part of the dwellers in the fens to allow the honour of being fen men to any but themselves. Happening to say that we were going to Kings Lynn, our friend remarked: "Oh, then you are going down to the fens." Afterwards, when we were in Cambridgeshire, and had told another inn acquaintance that we had come from Lincolnshire, we were met by the remark: "Oh, then you have been down among the fens."

It was a dark, wet, doleful night of that same day when, after journeying from Boston along the coast, through such scenery as we have already described, we found ourselves walking through the deserted streets of Kings Lynn to our inn in a wide-open square. It was as dismal a night as that memorable one, more than a century before, when, as Hood tells us—

> Two stern-faced men set out from Lynn,
> Through the cold and heavy mist,
> And Eugene Aram walked between,
> With gyves upon his wrist.

Kings Lynn, by the Ouse, with sloppy streets and down-pouring rain, was not a prepossessing picture, and the cheerful coffee-room of our inn, with a bright fire and a book, afforded a more comfortable lounging place than the great, dimly-lighted square outside. The town looked brighter on the morrow, when, in the early sunny hours, we strolled down to the quay to breathe the salt air and look out on the broad Ouse, dotted with craft and widening out in a dull, turbid way between low green banks to the sea. There was a group of sailors on the quay, and among them an ancient mariner, full of wise saws and friendly counsels, busy guiding the vessels in and out of harbour—a chatty, gossiping old salt, whose talk ranged from weather signs, the mysteries of navigation, the flight of birds, the identity of doubtful craft hovering about the river mouth, to the habits and customs of Dutchmen and other foreigners he had met with in his voyagings. Over the river the swallows were skimming and gathering as if for flight, but our mariner doubted that probability, remarking that there must first be the usual great gathering of the birds about the corn exchange in the market place, and a great chattering and general palaver, and that being over they would disappear suddenly, going no man knew whither. Kings Lynn is a pleasant town to ramble about. It has two great churches of noble architecture, and ruined traces of the abodes of friars of orders black, white, and grey. In its quiet and more secluded streets you come upon bits of ancientry, the waifs and strays of monastic times, or get peeps into the green courtyards of old houses with dormered red-tiled roofs overgrown with velvet-mosses and lichens, with vines upon the walls, glossy-leaved luxuriant shrubs in the areas, and bright, gay flowers in the window-places.

From Kings Lynn we took train along the flat, marshy coast of the Wash to Wolverton, from which, in a shower of rain, we ascended the high sloping common along a broad, grass-margined sandy road between fir plantations, through which we got glimpses of great stretches of full-flowered purple heather, and as we got up higher among sandy roads that dipped into wooded hollows and curved over undulating country, we could see below the common, and the firs, and the heather, the long, flat, dyke-intersected pastures dotted with slow-moving spots of cattle, and beyond them the salt marshes and the rainy sea. The road led to Sandringham, and having got a glimpse of the pretty church and the gables of the great house rising above the trees, we retraced our steps and took train for East Dereham.

Cowper is buried at East Dereham, and to reach it
we passed from the fens to a soil suggestive of chalk
and flint and then again to moister surroundings, to
green lanes, copses, farms, and villages of the kind
which one always associates with Cowper's landscapes.
East Dereham is a town of red brick houses and
shops, many of them being ranged about an open
market space in the centre, with long gardens behind
them. From this market place the streets straggle
out into green fields, showing avenues of gables and
roofs relieved by the swinging signboards of inns.
Opposite our inn, down one of these byways, is
the church of St. Nicholas standing among thatched
cottages, with a well-wooded park close by and
low-lying meadows behind. One of these thatched
cottages bears on its gable the date 1502. The church
has a square tower, and standing apart from it is
another bell-tower built of flint stone. In the churchyard is a stone which records the memory of Jean de
Narde, son of a notary public of St. Malo, a French
prisoner of war, aged twenty-eight years, who, having
escaped from this bell-tower, was pursued and shot
by a soldier on duty, Oct. 6, 1799. Not far from
this is a spring within the ruins of a baptistry which
once held the body of Withburga, youngest daughter
of Anna King of the East Angles. In 974 it was
stolen by the abbot and monks of Ely and buried in
the cathedral there. It was a cold, cheerless afternoon

when we stood beside Cowper's grave, which consists of an upright slab within a railed enclosure inside the church, and not far from Mrs. Unwin's. The church was chill and sombre, and there was a driving, drizzling rain outside. Near by our inn stood the house where Cowper and Mrs. Unwin died. It is now destroyed and a Cowper church erected on its site. It is said that much of the woodwork of the room in which Cowper died has been preserved in the new building. You may see the gable of it showing above the line of roofs to the left of the illustration.

From East Dereham we went to Yarmouth, taking Norwich on the way. Norwich is surrounded with gardens and orchards, and the freshness of the country penetrates its busiest streets. A beautiful river winds round it and the houses are clustered about a hill with a castle perched on it, from which you can look down upon an irregular mass of roofs and count the towers of nearly forty churches. The cathedral sends up its tall spire among them, and has beauties peculiar to itself, but did not impress us like Lincoln. It surpasses Lincoln, however, in its beautifully decorated cloisters, and the exterior view of the east end is very fine with its lofty clerestory of pointed windows supported by great flying buttresses.

The journey from Norwich to Yarmouth was through a lush, deep-pastured country, that flattened itself out to a dead level as we approached the sea. There are two Yarmouths, the old town and the new, crowded together on a peninsula between the river Yahr and the sea. It is at the old fishing town that you alight from the train, after passing along the shore of the reed-fringed Braydon water, and find yourself in a dense, irregular mass of buildings mixed up with the river and the ships. In this old town there are three or four parallel streets linked together with some hundred and fifty or more narrow rows or passages with houses on each side, in no case apparently more than eight feet wide. Threading your way across the main streets by means of these rows you get peeps into domestic interiors, and quaint nooks and corners, and see occasionally efforts to keep birds and plants and flowers alive in the close compact spaces. Beyond these rows there is a wide open space with trees and greenery, and a vast loftily-spired church at one end. Here commences the new town, stretching away in monotonous streets to the distant shore and the fine promenade extending in a long irregular line of buildings for two or more miles. Our inn was in the market place, and had a bow-windowed coffee-room in the upper story. It was a wild windy night, with a rough tumbling sea, as we walked for miles along the broad, dimly-lighted promenade and shore, and one remembers listening to music, along with a crowd of people gathered under a fluttering awning at the end of a dimly-lighted pier, amid the roar of the wind and waves.

MARKET PLACE, YARMOUTH.

YARMOUTH.

The morrow was stormy and we could see the vessels running in for shelter, and in the lifeboat house, where we had sought refuge, we listened in sight of the sea to a story of shipwreck and rescue recited in verse by a boatman with much dramatic vigour. Before we left Yarmouth we visited the great church, and were astonished at the vastness of its proportions and the beauty of some of its windows.

From Yarmouth we went to Lowestoft by rail, and at St. Olaves passed a strip of moorland, with gorse and heather, and clumps of firs, the sight of which was refreshing. We only got a peep at Lowestoft; built in the old part of it on a slope of cliff, with flights of stairs and gardens known as Scores, leading down to the gorse-tufted, close-cropped common land that borders the shore. Then we ran out again past Oulton Broad, and many other water spaces, to the Isle of Ely, arriving there after nightfall, and thinking the little cathedral city must be asleep or dead, so silent and deserted was it as we mounted the hill from the station, and passed along tree-bordered roads and by darkened houses and the great dim minster to our inn close by.

Awake but drowsy we found it next morning when we turned out early to look at the cathedral. Ely is a place for day dreaming. You feel that you are far away from the noise of the world's work. Strolling about it you come upon venerable houses and gardens, green spaces, and avenues of tall trees, and get sight of the flat country below in glimpses between them, or down some steep picturesque street, where you may see tall fuchsias hanging a drooping wealth of flowers above the window of some old-fashioned shop. The cathedral stands upon the hill, the houses and gardens are gathered about it on the slope, and the whole is encircled with the silence of the fens, where the deep-rutted roads give no sound of wheels, and the water in the dykes and the river is noiseless in its flow. In the cathedral we found a venerable grey-bearded verger in gown and skull-cap sitting meditatively by the gates of the choir. Presently we heard the sweet sounds of a hymn from some unseen corner, and, tracing it, came upon a dimly-lighted Norman chapel hid away in a recess of the nave, and behind a curtain a little group of early worshippers gathered about an altar. As Lincoln Cathedral exists in the memory as a monument of rich carving, Ely is associated with a lavish display of colour. Massiveness and majesty it has in its turreted towers and its magnificent nave, and complex beauty of styles in its architecture from Norman downwards; but it is the gold and colour that light up the choir, cover the roof of the nave, and the walls of the great lantern tower up to where the stained glass of its windows shine like jewels, that strike the beholder most. It would be useless to attempt to describe a building so full of beauty, and the charm of history and tradition. We met a man there who had visited it every year for fifteen years, and was still wondering and admiring. When we had seen the lady chapel, with its carvings all hacked and hewn by Cromwell's troops when they stabled their horses there, we left the minster and went down to the river, where

> Willows whiten, aspens quiver,
> Little breezes dusk and shiver,
> By the wave that runs for ever.

The Wen runs in a narrow channel now, but it must have had a wider waterway once, and probably flowed nearer the cathedral, otherwise one would doubt whether the singing of the monks could be heard by those who navigated its waters. One would be sorry to have the shadow of a doubt thrown upon that solitary fragment of a lost ballad which tells how

> Sweetly sang the monks of Ely
> As King Canute rowed by.

The fact is, we are told, that "the fens which surround the Isle of Ely constitute a vast alluvial flat, and must formerly have been a shallow bay six times as large as the Wash, which has been silted up by the deposits of the Wen, the Welland, the Witham, and the Ouse."

From Ely we went to Cambridge, and took up our quarters at one of its oldest inns, and roamed at our ease about colleges, quadrangles, cloisters, and gardens, for it was vacation time, and we were free to go where we pleased. In and out, we threaded our way through the venerable piles, leaving scarce one unvisited, crossing and re-crossing the Cam by graceful bridges, lingering often to look at the river, with the smooth shaven grass reaching to the water's edge, the willows, the tall elms, the shady avenues of limes, and all the other sweet surroundings of this nursery of learning which in its continued life through the centuries seems a realisation of the old Greek idea of beautiful and eternal youth everlastingly striving. May not one say of Cambridge what Mr. Matthew Arnold says of her sister Oxford, that "she is steeped in sentiment as she lies spreading her gardens to the moonlight . . . . by her ineffable charm she keeps ever calling us near to the true goal of all of us, to the ideal, to perfection, to beauty, in a word, which is only truth seen from another side."

From Cambridge we took our departure for Stamford, calling at Huntingdon on the way. Still through the flat fen lands, with alders and willows, and sedgy watercourses and high grasses, and rich cornlands and comfortable homesteads, we went, getting a peep at St. Ives and the slow-moving Ouse, with the narrow, steep old bridge over which Carlyle says Cromwell may have travelled; with a country about it of which he also says, "it has a clammy look, clayey and boggy, the produce of it, whether bushes and trees, or grass and sedges, gives you the notion of something

ELY.

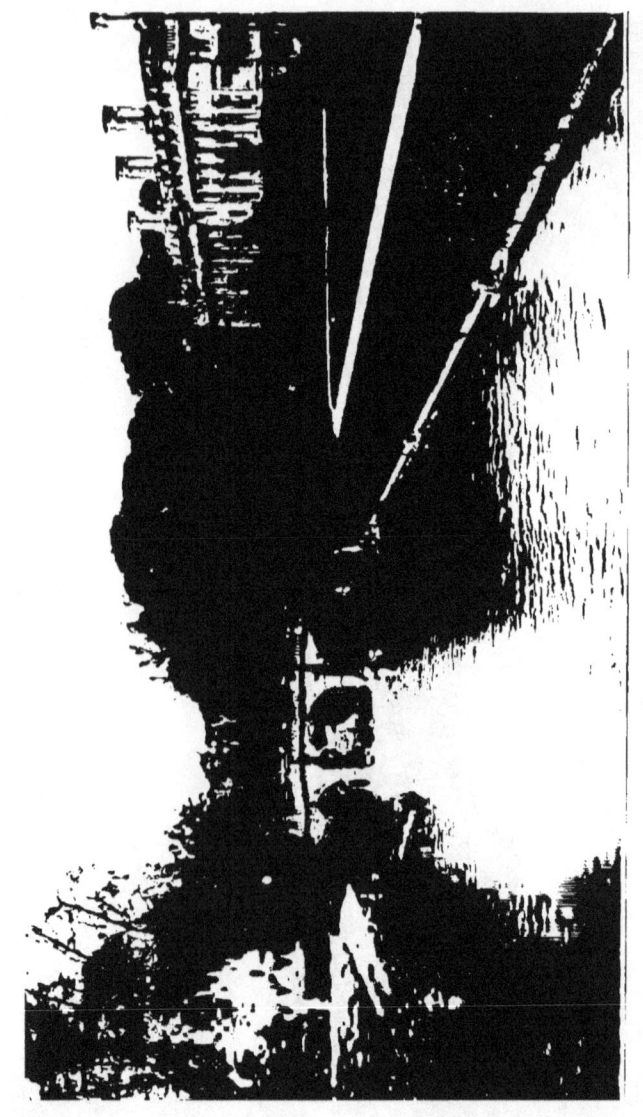

VIEW ON THE RIVER, CAMBRIDGE.

lazy, dropsical, gross." Pleasant, cheery, clean-looking Huntingdon lies on the edge of the fen country, and is almost emancipated from it. Gay flowers are cultivated on its window-sills, and when its one long street and market are thronged with busy farmer folk it has a bright, well-to-do, thriving look. We went to service in the church where Cromwell was baptised, and saw in the street opposite to it the fragments of Norman architecture, carefully preserved, which formed part of the school in which he was taught. From a worthy tradesman standing at his door close by we heard that story of the Protector, when a boy, being carried away by an ape to the leads of his uncle's house at Hinchinbrook. The house where Cromwell was born has been taken down, and another stands on its site, hid away behind a high wall and a ponderous gateway; but the house at Hinchinbrook is still standing, and we went to look at its gables and vanes visible above the thick belt of trees within the park fence. Then we bade good-bye to Huntingdon and the fen country, and taking train again ran on to Stamford, entering it by the Welland side in the purple gloaming, through which, above the river mist, the town loomed up darkly.

An interesting youth who helped to carry our luggage up to the hotel confided to us the information that there was a travelling circus in the town, having ideas of his own, no doubt, as to what we had come to

Stamford to see. Stamford and Stamford Baron, with their time-stained old stone houses, lie on each side of the river Welland, and are linked together with a fine bridge, leaning upon which you look upon picturesque alms-houses by the stream side, and rich meadows and uplands clothed with trees. Stamford stands on high ground, and looks down upon Stamford Baron, but for all practical purposes they form one town, which, though of moderate dimensions, has five fine old churches, and a history reaching back to dim Saxon days and beyond, and retains in names and stones traces of a castle, priories, friaries, and other bits of antiquity. It has been the scene of many royal displays and much fighting, retains many old customs, and in years gone by amused itself with bull-baiting. On market day you may see many fine tall men about, and in this connection be reminded that the celebrated Daniel Lambert lived here and is buried at Stamford Baron. Our inn was a building of vast proportions, and is said to have cost the modest sum of forty-three thousand pounds. It is built of stone with Corinthian columns, and is crowned with a statue of Justice, the work of a Royal academician. In this inn, with its long corridors, wide stone staircase, and spacious chambers relieved with old pictures and prints, and a statue or two, we rested for two nights, and in the interval visited Burleigh Park, with its grand avenues of trees, its deer, its glades and pastures, and its noble house, all associated with that romantic story of the landscape painter and the village maiden, which Tennyson's ballad tells so sweetly. We walked out to Oakham, getting on the way views of wide Rutlandshire vales, well wooded and fertile, extending to vague blue distances, and passing through the beautiful villages of Empingham and Whitwell. Through a wide tract of woodland and cornland, by Burley House on the Hill and its parkland, and along a silent, deserted road we came to Oakham. It has a great church, the remains of castle walls, and within them a queer little assize building where they hold civil and criminal trials in one hall, the judges facing each other, and the people interested occupying a space between. The interior walls are covered with horseshoes exacted from peers and royal personages who have driven through the town for the first time. Oakham concerns itself with corn and malt among things agricultural, and to the stranger has a peaceful, contented aspect.

From Stamford, through a fox-hunting county, by Melton Mowbray and Leicester, we passed into such midland scenery as George Eliot has made us familiar with, and halted at Nuneaton, where we found nothing more interesting than a large red-brick house in a quiet lane by the church, where we were politely shown the plain little schoolroom attached, where the great novelist was taught. From here we went to

Market Bosworth—a group of houses on a hill overlooking Bosworth Field, with a grammar school and a fine old church and close by it, within gilded gates, a manor house, with a great swelling parkland about it, with deer in it, and views over an extensive and wooded country. Of the inn, of its obliging host, and the homely hospitality dispensed to us, we have grateful recollections. One of the pleasantest memories of our journey is the little parlour where we sat by the fire and discoursed with our host of Bosworth Field, and read quaint and humorous old Hutton's history of the fight, which our host lent to us. In view of visiting the scene of the battle it was amusing to come upon such a passage as this: "Modern cultivation is a dreadful enemy to antiquity. The husbandman has with great labour destroyed the extent and appearances of these camps. I could not help smiling while I conversed with a farmer who resides on the verge of Richard's camp when he repeatedly cursed him for spoiling his land; and I asked him whether the shade of Richard might not with equal propriety curse him for spoiling his camp." On the morrow our worthy host placed a pony-carriage at our disposal, to take us, under the guidance of his son, to the battlefield. We drove along moist lanes and under dripping trees through a pleasant undulating country to a point on Redmoor, near three miles away, from which we walked across wet pastures to King Dick's Well, from which the king is said to have drunk before the battle. Walking over the scene of the fight, and trying to realise it from old Hutton's description, we indulged the pleasant fancy that the long ridges in the pastures might be the traces of Richard's lines, and that the little bit of unreclaimed bog in a hollow of the land was really the place where he was unhorsed and slain. It was wet work walking in the rain over that grassy land; and like Richard, before the battle, one felt constrained to say:

We would these dewy tears were from the ground.

Red-wet shod with rain and red clay we turned from the battle-field and took train close by, for Lichfield. There, with but an hour or two at our disposal, we made our way through picturesque streets of mellow red brick buildings, with old hostelries among them, and so to where the three tall spires of the cathedral rise above the willow-fringed minster pool and the venerable houses of the close. The west front is crowded with sculptured forms of prophets, priests, kings, and saints, and the interior leaves on the mind the impression of graceful beauty in arch and column, of sculptured marble, rich tabernacle work, and delicate tracery, rather than massiveness of proportion. Dr. Johnson and the cathedral divide the interest in Lichfield. It was his bust, placed beside that of Garrick, that we came upon first in the sacred pile; and it was to the museum that we went next to inspect such memorials of him as are there preserved; to the market place where his statue is, and the house where he was born; and, finally, to an old inn near it where we fain would believe he had sometimes sat.

For the rest our notes go on to record how from Lichfield we passed through Stafford to familiar Shrewsbury, where, in the clear shining after rain, we must needs pause again to look at the old timbered houses and the Quarry, and stroll by the Severn side in the soft evening light. After nightfall we passed out again, and, crossing the border, found ourselves at Welshpool, surrounded by the grand old mountains lifting their dark forms against a moonlit sky.

Scarce any space is left to tell of further wanderings—how we travelled over wild mountain ways, halting at Cann-Office among grouse shooters and anglers; how we went by Machynlleth and Corris to the lake of Tal-y-lyn, under Cadr Idris and by Abergwynolwyn, until at Towyn we saw the sea break on the shores of Cardigan Bay; how, following the coast, we walked to the mountain-guarded estuary of the Mawddach; and how, crossing the estuary by the long bridge, we came at last to Barmouth, with its sandy shore, its rock-perched houses, and crowds of visitors thronging its main street. There is no need to describe the place; the illustration here given will do better than words.

STAMFORD.

LICHFIELD CATHEDRAL.

BARMOUTH.

For convenience of departure we ran up to Corwen, where we rested for the last night of our holiday at an anglers' inn. Before leaving on the morrow we climbed the Berwyns among rocks and heather and fir woods, and looked down upon the valley and the winding Dee, and out over a multitude of mountain tops, an outlook in marked contrast with that far-off Lincolnshire fen country where our journey had begun.

TUNBRIDGE WELLS.

IN AN INN PARLOUR.

IT has been said that—

> All houses wherein men have lived and died
> Are haunted houses.

What is true of houses is, of course, equally true of inns. If you have travelled much, and are given to that retrospection which is the peculiar charm of travel, you will, doubtless, have many haunted inn chambers in the gallery of your imagination. How many shades of friends you have made merry with, and people you have met fill the rooms of the caravansaries where you and they

> Did bide your destined hour,
> And went your way.

Some of these places, too, are haunted by people whom we have known but have never met. If, for instance, you have ever slept in the Macbeth chamber of the inn at Stratford-on-Avon, you can scarcely have done so without seeing visions and dreaming dreams. Thackeray slept at Dessein's at Calais, and held converse with the ghost of Sterne, and though it was no longer the Dessein's of Sterne's time, so closely did the satirist identify the shade of the sentimentalist with the room which he called Sterne's that travellers still ask for it as for a haunted place. Dr. Johnson never could have visited that inn at Tunbridge Wells of which I am thinking now, because it is of more recent date than his time, but Thackeray may have done so, though I do not know that he ever did, yet both authors are associated with it for reasons which came about in this wise.

It was evening, dinner was over, and my travelling companion was dozing placidly in his easy chair, and I, more wakeful, was left to the companionship of my own thoughts, or to such books lying on the tables as the host had provided for his guests. We had arrived at Tunbridge at noon, intending to take a passing glance at the place, and then proceed on the morrow to the sea coast. In the meantime we had done such explorations as the time would permit. These had shown us that Tunbridge Wells is a pleasant place which straggles up and down hill, far and wide, in a cheerful careless way, about a high, breezy, sunlit common. This common is the special charm of the place. It rises to a height of several hundred feet above the sea level (you may read the exact figures on the front of the verandahed hotel perched on the highest point), and has gorse and brambles growing on it, and here and there great masses of rock breaking out from the green turf. From it you can look out upon innumerable villas dotted about the margin of it, or gleaming white from the wooded sides of the adjacent hills; and over the deep hollows that lie between, your eye is carried to purple distances. The common is crossed by paths and drives, and finger-posts show you the way to the great Toad Rock and other similar attractions. In the afternoon hours people ride, or walk, or drive along the ways; children and nursemaids are scattered over the turf; and old gentlemen seated on sunny benches doze over their newspapers, while the band makes music on the Pantiles below.

Our hotel was on the lower ground, and near the Parade and the famous wells. Across the road the common rose abruptly with some tall trees on the edge of it, and under these a line of hackney carriages were waiting for hire. The quaintest and most old-world part of Tunbridge is the Pantiles, or Parade, which consists mainly of a long row of many-gabled buildings, with a piazza running the length of it, and giving the tradesmen's shops somewhat the air of cloistered seclusion. Along the front grow tall shady trees, and across the way, and around, other buildings crowd and elbow each other irregularly, with the pump room standing detached at the end. In one corner of the piazza is the well, which, when I was there, was presided over by an elderly lady, who sold flowers and filled the beakers of those who came to drink, and who told you how many years she had, like a naiad, haunted this spring of healing waters. It was about these Pantiles that the old-world society gathered when the place was fashionable. Here they walked and danced and talked, and made merry over their cups to the sound of the fiddles, busy at work under the trees. The trees are still there, and the music is still played, but the company and the manners are changed. If you want relics of the quainter time you will find them not so much on the Pantiles as in old curiosity shops hereabouts, in the shape of pictures and furniture, possibly the waifs and strays of the wrecked households of people who once came there.

There was so little of the quaint old-world life to be seen among those who were moving about the tree-shaded ways, that in the seclusion of the inn parlour one had to conjure up the forms of those who had visited these Pantiles in the far-off years. One gets glimpses of the ancient manners in such books as Dr. Doran's *A Lady of the Last Century*, wherein the sprightly Mrs. Montagu describes some of the people she met there. She was astonished to find the grave Dr. Young and old Colley Cibber on the most intimate terms. Mrs. Montagu, walking on the Pantiles, asked the doctor how long he intended to stay, and his answer was, "As long as your rival stays!" When this riddle was explained, the "rival" proved to be the sun. The lively lady sketched the people who crowded the Pantiles: "Jews, Christians, and Heathens," she calls them. She says, "Lady Parker and her two daughters make a remarkable figure . . such hats, capuchins, and short sacks as were never seen! One of the ladies looks like a statebed running on castors. She has robbed the valance and tester of a bed for a trimming." She describes the vicar thus:—"The good parson offered to show us the inside of his church, but made some apology for his undress, which was a true canonical dishabille. He had on a grey striped calamanco gown; a wig that once was white, but by the influence of an uncertain climate, turned to a pale orange; a brown hat encompassed by a black hatband; a band somewhat dirty, that decently retired from the shadow of his chin; a pair of grey stockings, well mended with blue worsted, strong symptoms of the congenial care and affection of his wife, who had mended his hose with the very worsted she had bought for her own." The vicar was a smoker, too, it seemed, for she says, "I saw a large horn tobacco-box with Queen Anne's head upon it peeping out of his pocket."

Thackeray I have said came here; indeed he knew it well, and in that Roundabout Paper, called *Tunbridge*

THE PANTILES, TUNBRIDGE WELLS.
(From a Photograph by The Photochrom Co. Ltd. By permission.)

Toys, he tells us that it was familiar to him as a boy. Writing that paper, he says; "As I look up from my desk I see Tunbridge Wells common and the rocks, this strange familiar place which I remember forty years ago. Boys saunter over the green with stumps and cricket bats, other boys gallop by on the riding-master's hacks . . I wend my way to the Pantiles, the queer little old-world Pantiles, where a hundred years since so much good company came to take its pleasure. Is it possible that in the past century, gentlefolk of the first rank (as I read lately in a lecture on George II. in the *Cornhill Magazine*) assembled here and entertained each other with gaming, dancing, fiddling, and tea? There are fiddlers, harpers, and trumpeters, performing at this moment in a weak little old balcony, but where is the fine company? Where are the earls, duchesses, bishops and magnificent embroidered gamesters? A half a dozen of children and their nurses are listening to the musicians; an old lady or two in a poke bonnet passes; and for the rest I see but an uninteresting population of native tradesmen. I stroll over the common and survey the beautiful purple hills, twinkling with a thousand bright villas, which have sprung up over this charming ground since first I saw it. What an admirable scene of peace and plenty! What a delicious air breathes over the heath, and blows the cloud shadows across it, and murmurs through the full clad trees? Can the world show a land fairer, richer, and more cheerful?" They still make those Tunbridge toys of which Thackeray discoursed, as the familiar red-backed Directory will tell you, for therein you may read how "the trade of Tunbridge Wells is similar to that of Spa, in Belgium, and consists chiefly in the manufacture and sale of ladies' work-tables, boxes, toys, and fancy articles made of wood inlaid in mosaic, and called Tunbridge ware, the woods principally used for this purpose are beech, sycamore, holly, cherry, and plum, inlaid and beautifully polished: the elegance of these articles is universally admired, and their manufacture gives employment to a great number of hands."

Among the books, of the guide book type, lying on the table of the hotel parlour I found one in which the author, a well-known writer of light and trifling society verses, undertakes to revive descriptively in prose this old-world life of the Tunbridge Pantiles, but in a manner not so successful as Thackeray's. Among other notable things he tells us that here in his time, along with other distinguished persons, came Dr. Johnson, and this gives him an opportunity to write rather contemptuously of the great Cham of Literature, who seems to this later writer, to have been little more than a pompous, overrated, and ill-mannered pedant. Such an opinion of grand old Samuel in these days is calculated to startle one. One feels almost as much shocked as Miss Jemima Pinkerton, when, in disdain of the gift, Becky Sharp flung the dictionary of the great lexicographer at the feet of that lady as she drove from the school, which had been honoured with the worthy doctor's patronage. Of little moment, however, was the opinion of this literary trifler, but his reference to the doctor had brought another ghost upon the scene.

It was in 1748 when Johnson came to the Wells and met Garrick, and Richardson, and Cibber, and Mr. Pitt and others. They have preserved a sketch of these notabilities at Tunbridge, and foremost among these is the worthy doctor. One can recall in imagination that distinguished company with its wigs and lace and ruffles. In that year, as they walked the Pantiles, Johnson was hard at work on his Dictionary, "tugging at his oar," as Boswell says, and Richardson and his rival Fielding were busy, too, writing novels in their own respective ways.

It was rather odd that one should find also among the books on the table an old number of the *Contemporary Review*, with an article in it on Dr. Johnson, by the author of *Obiter Dicta*. Very seasonable and entertaining it was to read this article, written in that off-hand irresponsible vigorous way which marks Mr. Birrell's essays, and all the more pleasant because one could sympathise with the spirit which conceived it, and all that was said in praise and defence of honest and trusty Samuel. One could agree with him, too,

I

when he says, "Johnson's literary fame is in our judgment as secure as his character. . . 'Never,' as he wrote to Mrs. Thrale, 'let criticism operate upon your face or your mind, it is very rarely that an author is hurt by his critics. The blaze of reputation cannot be blown out, but it often dies in the socket.' Dr. Johnson is in no danger from anybody, none but Gargantua could blow him out, and he still burns brightly in his socket." And then he goes on to ask, "How long will this continue? Who can say? It is a far cry to 1985. Science may, by that time, have squeezed literature out, and the author of *The Lives of the Poets* may be dimly remembered as an old fellow who lived in the dark ages and had a very creditable faculty for making chemical experiments." Then followed some gossip about ghosts, with Johnson's opinion about ghosts in general, a subject not to be enlarged upon here.

By the time I had finished my magazine article, my travelling companion awoke, so I handed it over to him for his delectation, and, taking up my bedroom candle, passed away into another land of dreams.

SOME COMMERCIAL TRAVELLERS' SAMPLES.

I.

A Dantzic Traveller's Reports.

IT may perhaps not be accounted altogether out of place if among the samples of an uncommercial kind, which the present writer ventures to lay before his readers, there should be included some whose origin and characteristics are distinctly commercial. These samples, lying on the table before me, consist of written and printed matter, the products of various pens, the author in each case being a commercial traveller. The printed ones are in book form and have been published, but the manuscripts are of a more private nature. They are not of this time, the latest dating back about fifty years, and the earliest belonging to the middle of last century. Beginning with the earliest sample, it may be said that it is included in a scrap-book—now lodged in the Manchester Free Reference Library—made up of curiosities collected by the late Dr. S. Hibbert-Ware, and is described as "the remarks of a traveller for some Dantzig commercial house on the credit of merchants and others in the United Kingdom, on whom he had called to solicit custom for his employers." These reports appear in faded ink on six unequal scraps of torn and faded paper, and the first sheet is dated "Dantzig, Anno. 1758." This date is repeated on other sheets, and then we come upon a later one inscribed "Feb. 1762;" the rest are undated. From the dating of them one is led to suppose that the lists of names were furnished from Dantzic. Whether the traveller was a foreigner or not we have no evidence, neither does it transpire for whom he was travelling. The commodities offered appear to have been various, including flax, hemp, yarns, linens, ashes and timber. The towns visited are Banff, Perth, and Edinburgh, in Scotland; Wexford, Waterford, and Newry, in Ireland; and locally, Manchester, Liverpool, and Warrington. Under each town we have a list of persons called on with the traveller's comments attached. These are often quaint and curious, and for the most part detailed, but in the case of one Scotch town he summarises his information regarding thirteen firms existing there by reporting that "all are good and will settle credits in Holland, but are smugglers; it is therefore advisable that you execute no orders from any place in the North Country without credit settled in Holland." It is not

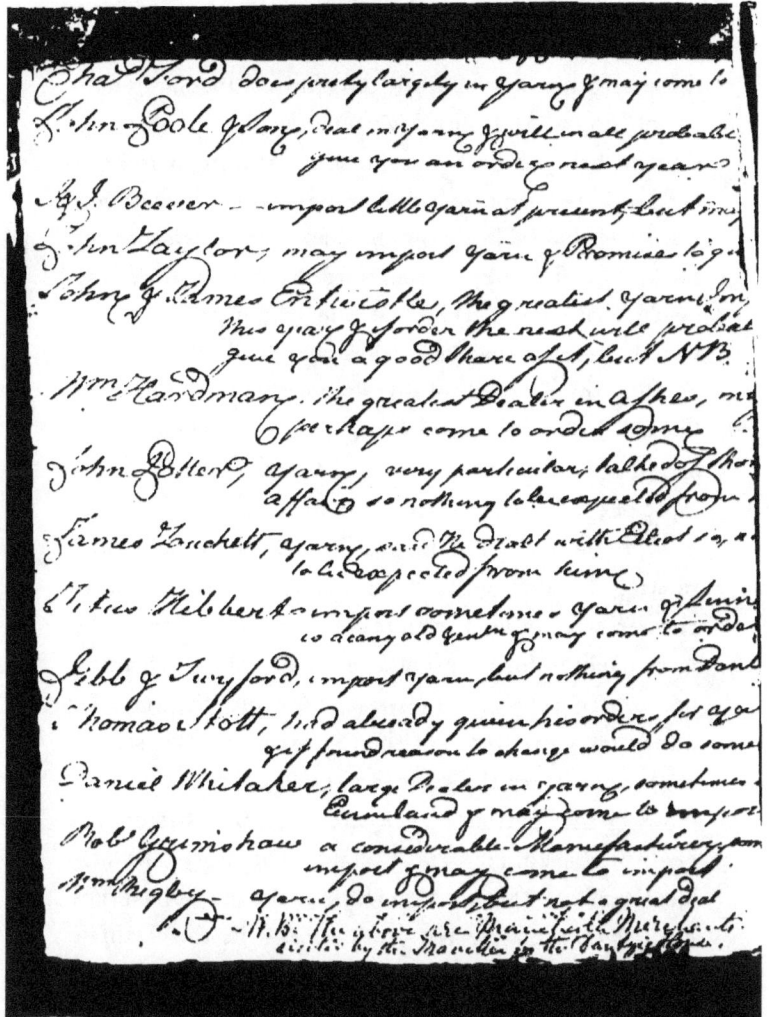

Fac-simile (reduced) of a portion of the Dantzic Traveller's Report relating to Manchester Merchants.

necessary to dwell at length upon our traveller's reports, but one notes in looking over them how, like those of other similar trade adventures, they are made up of hopes and disappointments, the prospective element being largely in evidence. He seems to have been a persevering man, for of one possible customer we find him telling how he has "called thrice but could not find him," therefore he has "talked the needful with his clerk." Of one whom he did interview he records the impression that he is "an active, bustling man, very proper for recommending our house." The most interesting feature about these scraps of paper is that one of them at least has, in the lapse of years, become a document of some importance in local history. The longest lists of names are those relating to Manchester and Liverpool, that of Manchester containing the names of forty-five firms who were likely to form business relations with the Dantzic house. In reporting of these, however, the traveller finds that some were not then in existence, the significant word "dead" being written opposite to them. Now, at that period, no Directory of Manchester had been published, for Mrs. Raffald's Directory, the first local book of the kind, did not make its appearance until 1772, probably ten years later. In this Dantzic traveller's report, therefore, we have been furnished with what appears to be, within its limits, the earliest accessible list of Manchester merchants.

II.

THE ADVENTURES OF JOHN KIGHLEY.

MY next samples are also in manuscript, but they are more voluminous and of an interest wider than the Dantzic traveller's scrappy memoranda. They are the journals of John Kighley, and consist of two books of unequal size, dealing with matters which occurred to him at different periods of his life. They came into my hands from different sources and at different times, and it was the larger and later-dated volume that I made the acquaintance of first. It is a neatly written manuscript, somewhat faded with age, and bound in brown and tattered covers, from which the leather is peeling in strips, giving the book the appearance of what Charles Lamb would have called "a ragged veteran." It was lent to me by Mr. W. S. Ogden, of Manchester, and is one of several manuscripts of a similar kind picked up by him when that rich storehouse of literary curiosities, the library of old John Jarmyn, now deceased, was broken up and distributed under the hammer of the auctioneer.

This gives an additional interest to the volume, for I knew John Jarmyn well. He was a mighty book-hunter and a well-known figure in old book shops. To possess books and accumulate them within every capacity of his means of storage was, outside his occupation as a lawyer, the absorbing passion of his life.

He had various storehouses for his books, not excluding his office, where he conducted his business among huge piles of them with little space left for himself, his clerk, and his clients. The storehouse that I knew best was his living room. It was an apartment crowded with literary treasures and antique curiosities of various kinds, so crowded in fact that the space which could be allotted to guests admitted of no more than a chair or two arranged about the fireplace. Books were in evidence everywhere, for the bookcases had long been filled to their utmost capacity, and the work of piling volumes on the floor in stacks had begun. There they stood like cairns, upon which John Jarmyn deposited his books as memorials of the immortal dead among authors, and within one of these piles, doubtless, the Journal of John Kighley lay imbedded until the disturbing hand of the auctioneer was laid upon it.

John Kighley was a commercial traveller of Leeds, and this journal is the record of two business journeys to America, the time covered by his narrative being from September, 1804, to May, 1807. The narrative proved so interesting on the first reading that the present writer was led to make a summary of it, which was afterwards printed in the *Manchester City News*. It is from this source that I propose to make such extracts in brief as will serve the present purpose. The first extract gives a general impression of the journalist, and is noteworthy because it afterwards led to the discovery of the earlier manuscript.

"From internal evidence of the journal," I then wrote down, "it is apparent that John Kighley was a travelled man, and one who had seen adventures. For instance, under date December 1st, 1804, he says: 'This day was the anniversary of my release from captivity; and I did not fail to remember the health of old Jugan.' Afterwards we come to learn that it was at Nantes he was confined a prisoner, and towards the close of his journal he tells us that in addition to this loss of liberty in France, he had been exposed to plague, pestilence, and famine, and to battle and shipwreck Possibly there may be in existence other manuscripts in which these matters are set down, for he seems to have been a man of an orderly and regular mind and predisposed to the keeping of a diary. In the present instance it is evident that he started out with a volume of blank leaves, and made his daily entries thereon in a very clear and succinct manner, and with very few erasures or corrections. The narrative is a curious mixture of private and business matters, observations on the weather, notes on passing events, and descriptions of what met the traveller's eye on land or sea, but interesting withal as affording us an illustration of the conditions under which a business man travelled at the beginning of the present century, together with some glimpses of

American life at that period. What was the exact nature of John Kighley's business is not very evident, but he seems to have gone over mainly to collect moneys due to his firm, and to arrange affairs in which the holding of land had a part. It may be remarked here, however, that he was evidently a very intelligent man, acquainted, too, with other languages than his own, as certain eruptions of French and German in his journal serve to show."

Now it happened that when this description of John Kighley's journal and the suggestion of the existence of other journals came under the notice of Mr. W. E. A. Axon, of Manchester, it occurred to him that he had in his possession an unsigned manuscript, relating to the writer's capture and imprisonment at Nantes, and on comparison it was found that the authors of the two journals were identical. The earlier diary, therefore, will serve as a sort of prelude to the later one. It is a small book with a grey cover, and pages of note paper size. The first date in it is June 13th, 1797, and under the pious heading "Dieu me soit en aide!" the writer tells how, on this day, in the evening, he goes on board the "Eunice," Captain Seal, a vessel of 220 tons, mainly laden with salt, and then lying about four miles from Liverpool, meaning to sail to Philadelphia as soon as the wind will serve. The next day this is effected, the anchor is weighed, and the traveller gets fairly under way with his journal, where we have the finny Monsters declined hostilities, wheeled about, and fled from us, to the great disappointment of all lovers of Sport. Distance run p. Log, 93 Miles.

July 7. Friday, 1797. Nothing particular having occurred since Tuesday, I now come to the most eventful period of my whole life, wh. is our life then our Capture by a French Pirates from Nantes called the Intrepide Cap.n Cadeau a Brigg of about 100 Tons mounting 14 Guns and about 80 Men. we fell in with her about 9 oClock in the Morning, when she ordered our boat to be got out & the Captain to go on board with his Papers, after he had been gone some time the Lieu- tenant of the French Ship returned for the rest of his Papers, and we anxiously wall- ed the event, having at the same time a suspicion of its being a French Ship, tho' she then carried English Colors, when our Captain had been aboard about half an hour, she suddenly struck the English an hoisted French Colors, we immediately judged ourselves to be captured, and we were

Fac-simile Page (reduced) of John Kighley's Journal relating to his captivity in France.

accounts, not to be detailed here, of the incidents of the voyage. The progress is slow by reason of contrary winds, which necessitated much tacking; the sea too is often rough, and the voyager has frequently to write himself down "sick." Among his varying experiences, John Kighley, with an open-eyed wonderment, sets down as an interesting episode the advent of a school of porpoises, describing how the playful porpoise disports himself "by leaping forwards out of the water, and like John Gilpin, of equestrian fame, in the wash at Edmonton, throws it about most astonishingly." The next entry to this, however, has reference to an incident which proved a much more serious subject for astonishment. Under date July 7th he says: "I now come to the most eventful period of my life, which is no less than our capture by a French privateer from Nantes, called the "Intrepide," Captain Candeau, a brig of about 100 tons, mounting 14 guns and about 80 men. We fell in with her about nine o'clock in the morning, when she ordered our boat to be got out, and the captain to go on board with his papers. After he had been gone some time the lieutenant of the French ship returned for the rest of his papers, and we anxiously waited the event, having at the same time some suspicion of its being a French ship, though she then carried English colours. When our captain had been aboard about half an hour she suddenly struck the English and hoisted French colours. We immediately judged ourselves to be captured, and we were shortly after confirmed in our suspicions by seeing a number of her crew get into our boat, then alongside, who immediately after boarded and took possession of our ship. The lieutenant told us our private property should be respected. We then got our trunks, bedding, &c., which with ourselves were safely put on board the "Intrepide." Cato, the black cook, with the cabin boy, were ordered to remain on board, which injunction they reluctantly complied with. The captain has behaved with the greatest politeness to me, seating me at his right hand at dinner, drinking my health, &c. We have had an excellent dinner and several sorts of wine, with figs and raisins for the dessert; in short the treatment we have all experienced has been the most civil imaginable considering the circumstances we are in. The ship has been out 44 days, has taken four prizes, and is now bearing away for Nantes."

So courteous is our captain that we have hopes of obtaining a parole and of getting into Germany, and so to Munich or Frankfort. In spite of this, however, our people are not unsuspected of an intention to seize the privateer; our luggage is examined in search of weapons, and the officers and crew are under arms all night; two large swivels, loaded with grape shot, are fixed near the hatchway and men stationed near them.

This suspicion seems to last but for a time, and then we get along pleasantly enough with the captain who is a very sensible gentleman, who has read a good deal and speaks some English. He sailed round the world with the great Bougainville, when very young, acting as his secretary. His ship is one of the swiftest sailing privateers in France, and he has taken many prizes in addition to ours. We are now sailing for Nantes, and hope to reach there in eight days. On our way we overhaul several vessels and are in a continual state of alarm, as the privateer always prepares herself to fight any vessel she sees, the guns being run out, all hammocks got up and put in the nettings to form a shelter against small arms. On one day a ship of war makes down upon us, but as she misses stays twice we gain an advantage, and after a chase in which we crowd all sail, she gives up, and we get clear away. Our sailors are very patriotic, and are constantly singing "Ça Ira," the "Carmagnole," and other airs of the like kind. The officers, too, sing us several of their songs.

In due time, after various adventures, we near the coast of France and the mouth of the Loire, where there is a scare, one of our officers mistaking the towers upon an island there for two English frigates. Soon we sight Isle Dieu, with its fort and village and windmills, and then the coast line is revealed, very welcome to behold, but ah, that it had been America instead! Sad it is, too, to see at the mouth of the river a captured British ship carrying twenty-two guns, with a valuable cargo and seventy passengers—mortifying is it to see the English colours reversed. Very beautiful is the country hereabouts, with its gently rising hills, its cornlands and meadows, but as we sail up to Painboeuf, we note ruined villages, which have suffered from the "Brigands" in the war of La Vendee. The peasants are getting in both their hay and corn harvest at Painboeuf, where our captain is taken on shore. We get leave also to go, and pleasant it is to feel the solid earth again after thirty-four days on water. The officer who accompanies us is a very civil young man, and takes us along the narrow ill-paved main street, where tricoloured flags are hanging from pothouses, where the crews of privateers are carousing. He shows us the whole of the town and the places where the "Brigands" attacked it and were driven out by the Republican troops. This is the seventeenth of July, and to-morrow we go to Nantes. All the day we have had Custom-house officers on board, who we suspect are great villains, and against whom it is necessary to be on guard. Some of the crew, too, have got their friends from the town on board, and they are all getting drunk and insubordinate, and in these circumstances we stand a chance of being plundered. At night, when the officers have turned in, we keep a lamp burning in our cabin and a sharp look out lest the villains should rob us, and indeed, while the officers have been sleeping one ruffian has been ransacking our cabin for wine, provisions, and other property, which he has transferred through the port hole to a boat lying alongside.

Here, with the remark "pleasant warm weather," the journal comes to an end. How John Kighley fared in prison at Nantes is not told. Perhaps the conditions there were not favourable to keeping a journal. However, on another page we find a chronicle of dates which shows that he arrived at Nantes on the 18th July, and left it on the 20th September, when he was sent to St. Malo, and subsequently to Dinan. Eventually, on the 27th November, he left St. Malo, and travelled homewards by Guernsey and Portsmouth. He arrived in London on December 1st, and at Leeds on the 23rd of the same month, in time at least for making merry there at Christmas over his blessed release from captivity.

Turning now to that other record of his journeyings we find that it is on September 10th, 1804, that John Kighley leaves Leeds in the mail coach, and arrives at Liverpool at half-past seven in the evening, taking up his quarters at the King's Arms, in Water Street. He has business to transact here, consisting of receipts and payments, among the latter being one of thirty-five guineas to Captain Briggs, of the "Annawan," for his passage to America, twelve pounds of that sum being "for provisions and water," other stores to be provided by himself. Among these other stores which he lays in are five dozens of Burton ale and five dozens of cider, the bottles being included in the charge of ten shillings and sixpence per dozen, because, as he says, they cannot be returned. There is some delay between the engagement of his passage and the sailing of the ship, which it seems has managed to be "neaped by the tide."

After sundry visits to the ship, where he makes the acquaintance of the steward, who is a black man, and after delay by winds, embarkation and disembarkation, at last on September 17th, along with other cabin passengers, he is rowed some miles down the river, and getting on board sail is set, and the ship proceeds on her way. All goes well until the Isle of Man has been sighted and the Skerries light passed, when a head wind springs up by reason of which they can do nothing all the next day "but stretch backwards and forwards from the Welsh to the Irish shores." They have thirty-six persons on board, six of these being cabin and fifteen steerage passengers. After more head winds they get at last into the Atlantic Ocean and pleasant weather. Henceforth John Kighley gives, day by day, as far as possible, the latitude and longitude of the ship's situation, with the number of miles accomplished, and shows by his frequent use of

K

nautical phrases that he is not unfamiliar with navigation. He is very pleased with the sailing powers of the ship, and proud that with fewer sails she is able to keep her course as well as a companion vessel. the "Mississippi," which bears them company for a while, and is sometimes so close that jokes can be exchanged between the passengers.

But by-and-by another vessel comes in-sight which is not so attractive because she has the appearance of a French ship of war and fires two shots at the peaceful merchantmen, who hoist their colours, but cannot make out those of the stranger, which are shown in the mizzen peak. The glass shows, however, that she is "very long and rakish (as the sailors say) with the side next us painted red." As a precautionary measure those of the passengers who have papers of importance hand them to Captain Briggs. There is much speculation as to the intentions of this doubtful craft, which appears to be trying to overhaul them, but the ships are kept on their way, and so in time the intruder is lost to sight. Very soon after, however, another warlike vessel appears upon the scene, and "just after supper she gave us a shot when we hove to, as well as our consort, the stranger saying that he should send his boat on board, which he immediately did with two officers, who came down into the cabin and required to see the logbook. They inquired if we had seen any privateers, as they had information of some being hereabouts. We told them what we had seen and informed them which way she had steered. They hoped to give a good account of her and politely wished us a good passage. Their ship was the 'Nimrod' sloop of war of twenty guns, Captain Oker. After all this bustle we did not fail to celebrate Saturday night by drinking the healths of sweethearts and wives."

Under these fair weather conditions, with porpoises to play about the ship, sick passengers become well again, and do justice to the good dinners which are provided, whereat are discussed soups, boiled fowls, beef, roasted ducks and geese, plum puddings, and the rest, "with frequently a song and a segar after it." But there are times when sailing is not a joyous thing, and one reads of squally weather in which sails are split, the ship going through the water like an arrow, sometimes to be struck by seas which produce much disturbance among trunks, chairs, and crockery-ware in the cabin, and make sleep in the night an impossible thing. Then when the storm is ended we sleep soundly again "and dream of distant friends." Our case at the worst is not as bad, however, as that of a ship we meet, whose captain and nine men out of fourteen have been so sick that for a time they could not come upon deck. We have a scheme for passing letters on board this ship by tieing them to potatoes which are to be flung on board as she passes under our stern, but this is rendered unnecessary by our boat being sent to them in response to a request for a few candles. It is found, too, that other things are needed besides candles, and so the boat is sent a second time with "a bag of potatoes, together with some ale, porter and wine, which we are all glad to have in our power to furnish them with, and which are very thankfully received by them."

The good ship has many ups and downs, and there is much bad weather encountered, including fogs as land is being approached. At last, after a night of tossing in which we have not been able to sleep a wink, a clear morning dawns, with the wind favourable for steering to the mouth of the Delaware, and, more cheering still, at noon Dick, a black seaman, going up aloft, sees land on the lee bow, which said land we find is very distinguishable from the deck when we come up there after dinner. Pleasant is the sight of that shore with its fringe of trees, but not just yet to be reached though we take a pilot on board, and a gentle breeze carries us to the bay over which "the sun sets in a grand style." After sailing past the lighthouse it is too dark, however, for the pilot to distinguish the buoys, so that we have to cast anchor in a wind which freshens to a heavy gale, and the strain is so great that the windlass is broken, and we have to secure cables to the main mast.

During the night the gale becomes a hurricane, and we have a terrible time. The ship is blown from her anchorage, and to save her from wreck the captain puts out to sea again, the landing at Delaware having to be abandoned. And now John Kighley, who was a devoutly-minded man, says, "Here I would acknowledge the hand of Providence in this miraculous escape from shipwreck. O God, Thy hand was here! Not unto us but unto Thee ascribe we all."

At sunrise next morning the ship presents a sorry appearance after her distresses. "Poor 'Annawan'! how are the mighty fallen! so stately in all thy splendour, with top-gallant sails, studding sails, and sailing along with the swiftness of an arrow! What a contrast now! The mizzen mast and all its sails gone, the main top-sail and yard lost overboard, and the running rigging cut all away, the decks encumbered with the remains of the two cables and fragments of rigging." In fact, the poor "Annawan" has much the appearance of a wreck as we make our way for New York, "to which place may God send us a safe passage."

This consummation so devoutly to be desired is helped forward by a friendly ship which, having noticed our distress bears down to us, and after learning our condition, gives us a hawser and an anchor, but we make little way the wind having fallen again. Moreover, the fog comes down upon us presently, rendering of no use the light we hang in the fore-shrouds at night, hoping to get another pilot on board. So wearisome is the situation that "the captain and indeed, all of us begin to be very impatient; we almost think we shall have as much difficulty in making our port as ever Ulysses had." After this night of fog and a dead calm, however, the fog clears away under a light wind, and we can hear the sound of the surf on the shore, and some fishing boats come in sight. The appearance of the fishing boats is hailed as a deliverance, because if we are out much longer we shall be short of provisions; so we passengers are determined if possible to get on shore, and to that end we signal to the boats by hoisting an ensign under the sprit sail yard and firing a musket several times. Soon a boat is alongside, and we arrange for our shoreward passage, other boats coming to our relief, and in all these we wearied sea-travellers get ourselves stowed, saying good-bye to the "Annawan" for the time being; and after rowing four or five miles we are all landed, the women and children being safely beached without wetting from the surf, which is running high and with a loud roaring. Our feelings on finding ourselves once more on terra firma are not to be described, and we thankfully pay the modest sum of a dollar each for our shoreward passage. We find that the place of our landing is in the township of Shrewsbury, New Jersey, and here at a comfortable boarding-house, half a dozen of us take refuge, and over an excellent dinner of ham rashers, eggs, boiled fowls, and different kinds of vegetables, for which we are charged the modest sum of three shillings each, we enjoy ourselves very much, and talk of past difficulties overcome. It was on the seventeenth day of September that we sailed from Liverpool, and our voyage has been brought to this unexpected but happily safe ending on the thirtieth day of October.

From this place our traveller makes his way to Philadelphia, and then begins the serious business of the journey, in which John Kighley finds that, in some cases, his money settlements are not easily made, mean evasion of his presence being even resorted to. Social nights are pleasantly mixed up with commercial transactions, and old acquaintances and friendships revived, for our friend has been here before in 1801. So it comes about that on the evening of the day after his arrival, he having supped and stayed until a few minutes after twelve o'clock, his host insisting upon an extra segar, he finds when he gets to the hotel that the doors are closed upon him, and the inmates not to be awakened by very much knocking. There is nothing for it apparently but to walk about the city all night; "but about two o'clock," he says, "in the market house I met with a country farmer, who was looking after his wares along with many others, this being market day morning. He offered to take me to a house close by, where I might sit by a good warm stove till daylight. We went together, and found about twenty or thirty other farmers and market people, some drinking-beer, others singing or telling stories."

In the prosecution of that business which is the object of his American journey, and consists mainly in the settlement of accounts, John Kighley meets with much discouragement. There is a dearth of money in the country in the year of grace, 1804, and some of his merchant friends are dilatory and procrastinating. In one case the debtors express such great sorrow that the account should have been kept open so long, and make so many trite observations that John suspects the house is very much accustomed to dunning visits. He is desired to "call in the afternoon at four o'clock," and an endeavour will be made to settle the account. A good many afternoons, however, are destined to pass before that desirable settlement can be obtained, for they propose such shameful terms in the way of long-dated bills, that he has serious thoughts of going to law in the matter, but on reflection he abandons this method of collection, as he does the charge of compound interest, which is resisted in the final settlement. The collector of accounts has, it seems, to proceed with caution if he would succeed, especially in Virginia, whither John has to travel on this errand. He says: "A merchant here, when he wishes to receive his money from his customer (generally speaking) is obliged to use gentle language; to coax him to do his duty, for a suit has no terrors to him. If you remonstrate or threaten him, it is not uncommon for him to say, 'I'll run you the heats,' that is, he will stand a trial, and carry it from one court to another for years. Would this,' he asks, 'be the case were the legislative body of the State composed of a majority of merchants instead of lawyers?'" There are pleasanter phases, however, as when he tells us that he has settled an account with a debtor and dined with him afterwards, and spent a merry and musical evening; or as when he inserts in his journal a memorandum to the effect that he has found some of his customers the honourable and upright gentlemen he had always supposed them to be.

Up to now, however, our traveller's luggage is not to hand. It was on the 30th of October that we left the "Annawan" to pursue her crippled course to New York, taking with her our baggage, and it is not until the 27th of November that we hear certain tidings of her arrival at Philadelphia, though we have made frequent enquiries, and gone down to the Point to watch for her coming. To-day, however, returning from another outlook, we stumble upon Captain Briggs, who says he arrived with his vessel overnight. We go on board, and find the good ship looking as well as ever again. Later on we get our baggage entered at the Custom-house, and obtain the due permit to land it, all of which is accomplished in the civilest manner possible. For, says John, "the officer on board did not give me the least trouble. I merely unlocked my trunk, opened the lid, when he said, 'That's enough!' The officers here are a much more respectable set of men than those in England, or perhaps in any other country." This satisfactory business accomplished we dine at a friend's house upon canvas-backs, a kind of wild duck which is found in great abundance upon the rivers Susquehanna and Potomac, and are very fine eating.

Business engagements necessitate some travelling, and so journeys have to be taken to Baltimore and Alexandria. At the former place, to which we travel by the "Pilot" stage coach, we meet, at a dancing assembly, Madame Buonaparte, dressed quite à la Parisienne, and hear that Jerome is sick and confined to his room, the poor man having met with many disappointments in his attempt to leave the country. There is quite an elegant display of beauty at this ball, and we are much pleased with the taste shown by the ladies in their dresses. Both sexes dance extremely well, but they are fonder of cotillons than country dances, of which only two are danced. About eleven o'clock we have supper, and a little after twelve the greater part of the company has left the rooms. At Baltimore, too, we meet with three Indians on their way to Philadelphia. One is of the Chicksaws and the other two of the Catawbas. With these children of the forest we make friends by means of segars and punch and the gift of a coin each, which is to be treasured as a keepsake. So friendly do we become with each other that one of them, says John, "told me that if I was to travel through their country they would furnish me with whatever I might want, for nothing, and feed my horse as well as myself."

In turning over the pages of John Kighley's faded manuscript one comes to have a personal interest in the adventures of that honest commercial traveller, but though one would fain linger over details in which his pleasant peculiarities are revealed, the exigencies of space forbid. Interwoven with his narrative there is a curious story of the discovery, in his travels, of a long lost brother under conditions of a romantic kind, but this must be left untouched, nothing more remaining to be done than to glance rapidly at a few salient features of this narrative and so bring it to an end. He goes to Washington and sees President Jefferson there, visits the House of Representatives, too, and expresses his opinion freely respecting the said Representatives. The closing days of the year 1804 find him sojourning in Virginian Alexandria, and the final day of that year, besides its own important business transactions, brings thoughts of a grave kind and is not allowed to pass without this reflection. "We are now at the last day of the year, and when I look back, I see how eventful it has been to me, and how much reason I have to be grateful to the Great Power who has protected me at home and abroad. My transgressions have been many, and the mercies of Him who made me immeasurable." Then, on the morrow, we have "The commencement of a new year. 'May that Being who has hitherto protected me continue His gracious protection through the course of this, as well as to all my dear friends and relatives in whatever parts of the globe their lot may be cast.' The weather is of Arctic severity, but the cheerfulness of a coal fire and the company of friends compensates somewhat. At one of our evening visits we meet with a Mrs. Douglas, a lady who is of the Randolph family of this State, and is a lineal descendant of the Indian Princess Pocahontas, the daughter of Powhattan, who is mentioned by different authors, who have written accounts of the first settlement of Virginia. Mrs. Douglas and her children have something of the Indian features."

When we have transacted as much business as possible in Alexandria, we take our leave of it for Baltimore by the mail stage. The journey is a very cold one, and conducted in part through the night, with a continual irritating jolting, but we have for a fellow-passenger a gentleman who is a native of Canada, but who has resided in France. He is a very good companion, and tells how he has served in Italy as a conscript and fought at Marengo and Lodi, and elsewhere. At Baltimore we receive an invitation to dine at Mr. Buchanan's, in distinguished company

Jan.y 1805

the river after dinner I set off with Mr ... intending to walk part of the way with him to George town, but soon after we had got out of the town we were overtaken by some empty sleighs which had been with loads of lime wood we agreed with one of the drivers for a ... taken as far as he was going which was about 8 ... les accordingly we embarked or rather stepped upon it for it only consisted of two rough pieces of wood shaped like a skate iron which are connected by two cross bars making the width of the sleigh about so but at each end to these cross pieces of timber there is an ... fixed by fixing ... or some twisted twigs to each ... here the driver has a seat to ride upon when he has sold his load, when the hinder seat was all ... seated it was astride in the middle & hold on by the drivers seat, the roads being covered with snow of very hard we had a very pleasant passage & I walked back to town before sunset. Our appearance was something like the sketch beneath & we both agreed we should have made a figure in Europe

10th Frost still continues very keen the ice in the river very thick & hundreds of people upon it skating.
11th It possible this day was colder than the day before yesterday & it seems likely to continue. Saw Mr R. M. Scott who informed that S. would be here in a day or two. Spent the evening at Mr Wiltons. When I returned home sat up till after 1 oclock to see an eclipse of the moon which began about that hour & was total, however it

Fac-simile Page (reduced) of John Kighley's Journal relating to his American journeys.

which includes Jerome Buonaparte, to whom we are introduced by Mr. Buchanan, Mr. Cannes, his secretary, M. Garnier, his physician, Mr. Paterson, his father-in-law, and numerous other guests. Our experience of Jerome on this occasion is very favourable. "He is quite the gentleman in his manner and very unassuming." In person, "he is thin and delicate his complexion pale, and he is rather sickly in appearance." Upon the whole, we come to the conclusion there is a great resemblance between him and his brother in France, if one may judge from portraits. The dinner is a sumptuous one, and we have excellent madeira, claret, and champagne. Moreover, we find ourselves seated at table next to the secretary and physician, with whom we have pleasant talk. This feasting, it should be understood, does not in any way interfere with the serious business upon which we are engaged, for there are important settlements to arrive at if possible.

At New York, to which we proceed later, there are many social pleasures, and in one case only to be productive of regret, the cause being stated with that honest ingenuousness which characterises John Kighley's journal, of which let this entry be witness, " I had thought this morning to have cut out this leaf, not liking the appearance of what I wrote yesterday. However, upon further consideration, I have concluded to let it remain, as it may serve as a memento of my folly in drinking more wine than I ought to have done, and in direct violation of the resolution I had formed when I went." But in contrast with this there are many quiet evenings at home, when as we write up our diary and our thoughts fly homewards we can almost fancy we hear the bells of Trinity Church, Leeds, ringing a melodious peal, and when, other duties performed, we find great pleasure in reading from the British classics. How John Kighley visited Boston, and many other places, how he found his way back to Philadelphia, and of a multitude of incidents and events that occurred to him in moving accidents by flood and field, it is not possible here to tell.

On the 10th of July we embark on the "John Morgan" for England. We have a good voyage home, and on the 3rd of August land again in Liverpool, from whence we are not long in making our way to Leeds, there to meet with our friends once more. Our business engagement is now at an end, but, alas, it has brought no personal profit, and here we are, comparatively speaking without a shilling, "after twelve years' servitude, during which time we have been four times abroad, and have been exposed to plague, pestilence, and famine, to battle and shipwreck, and loss of liberty in France." However, we are hopeful, and when just now, the fear of invasion being strong in the land, we are called out to act as lieutenant of volunteers, we gladly respond, and in the highest spirits at the prospect of active service, declare, with our compatriots, that "we will acquit ourselves like men and Britons, who fight for all that renders life desirable." There is happily no need for this, and so we enter upon new and very promising business relations, which require us to sail away again to America.

Of that voyage—lasting from the 3rd of October to the 12th of December—full of interest though it is, in its distress and privations, we being obliged to live for fifty days on bread and water, and being otherwise so ill-used by our captain that we are well nigh mutinous—of all these things nothing more can be detailed here. Neither of our adventures during the period of our travelling in America, which lasted until April, 1807, can anything be said. Of the homeward voyage only can a word be given. This is taken in His Majesty's brig "Manchester," a beautiful little craft of 190 tons, mounting ten six-pounders, and in her on the 4th of April we sail from New York to Falmouth. On the 7th of May we pass the Lizard and the Manacles, and haul up in Falmouth harbour. Who shall express the delight we experience in seeing the English shores again, and the green fields "of that country which contains the dust of one's ancestors and the living objects of one's affections." How delightful it is to see "the beautiful green turf, studded here and there with tufts of furze in full flower of the richest yellow, where the nibbling flocks do stray."

With no more delay than is necessary after landing, we take the mail for London, where we sleep at a coffee house in Ludgate Hill, and are woke up by the booming bell of St. Paul's next morning. But our rest is not here, for we are bound to Stansted, in Essex, where we have relations, certain Talbots, of whom we have thought much in our travels. So we take coach to Bishop Stortford, passing through Epping Forest, and a charming country, and finish our journey in a postchaise, which sets us down in the evening "at the place where we have long wished to be."

III.

"A Veteran Highwayman."

This playful description of himself is given by a commercial traveller, who, sixty years ago, published anonymously some hints to his fellows of the road, and to whose little gilt-edged book relating to home travels —with "fourth thousand" on its title-page in testimony of its popularity—I now turn as a change from the strange adventures of John Kighley. In this case the author, like the needy knife-grinder, has no story to tell, but rather assumes the rôle of the friendly adviser. He takes the young commercial by the hand, as it were, and essays to train him up in the way he should go. To this end he discourses variously on the dignity and importance of commercial travelling; the education, personal requisites, and habits best adapted for the vocation; the etiquette, manners, and customs pertaining to the commercial room, together with many other things conducive to a reputable and successful life on the road. One is not concerned here to follow the veteran in detail through his sage counsellings, but, by way of illustration, may quote a little of his advice to the aspiring young traveller who is in danger of becoming what Carlyle would call a "dandiacal body." The subject is the one of dress and deportment, and our veteran delivers himself thus: "Far be it from us to question the importance of appearance, dress or manner. We are ourselves waxing somewhat ancient and gouty, and therefore speak of the foibles of some of our younger contemporaries more in sorrow than anger, and certainly without a particle of envy. We only wish them to hold these matters at just their real value. Every traveller should be well dressed, rather above than below the average standard, but he should eschew finery altogether. There is no excuse for his being badly dressed, as the world of tailors is wide before him where to choose, and if he cannot get fitted in one town he may in another; of course he should be scrupulously clean in his person and linen; the keeping a supply of the latter always ready for use is from the limited quantity permitted by his portmanteau a matter of some ingenuity. Three new coats in the year are necessary at the lowest calculation. As to appearance, of course Chesterfield's often repeated truism that 'a pleasing one is a letter of recommendation,' is doubtless incontrovertible, but we hold this to be one of the secondary requisites for commercial travelling. Let any commercial Adonis who has a distressing consciousness of the perfection of his outward man, qualify his self-admiration by remembering that when he presents himself at the door of a shop or counting-room smiling, alive to his fascinating powers, the master of that shop or room is frequently more occupied by calculating if the fine gentleman before him can supply him with goods at any increased advantage, than in attending very minutely to the gentleman himself. . . . Our own observation has led us to the opinion that the more quiet a traveller is in his dress and the more natural in his manner, the greater are his chances of success. The easiest way of pleasing is to be really yourself. . . . We would suggest the following hints to the young traveller in reference to this subject: Do not appear the *fine* gentleman for two reasons; 1st, Because shopkeepers are in general quiet people, and cannot approach such a phenomenon further than feeling somewhat uneasy while in contact with it; 2ndly, As it does no service, avoid such a gratuitous piece of acting. Do not fall into the other extreme of dressing slovenly and adopting the manners of a bear garden. The first shows a want of self respect, and the other a want of respect for your customers." When the veteran, in the process of his pilotage, brings the youthful traveller to the commercial room, and having asked him to take off his hat as he enters that privileged area, he is careful to make him acquainted with the various rules and regulations obtaining there, especially in matters relating to meals. Among these the dinner is the most important function with many features of interest and points of etiquette attached to it which require lengthened explanation. So the youthful tyro is instructed regarding the order of the dishes, the nature of the wines which accompany them, and of the interchange of courtesies effected through that medium when the president, vice-president, and indeed all the members of the company "take wine" with each other. He is instructed, too, regarding after dinner toasts and sentiments, and cannot fail to be impressed with the veteran's description of the functions of the dinner president of that antique time. Says the guide "while the president is in office he is the representative of the wants and wishes of the company. He it is that issues all the orders that concern the commonwealth, and should any unwary tapster attempt to introduce japan ink upon his table under the name of port, it is the president's province to rate the delinquent, which he generally performs in the true spirit of fat Sir John, who, if we mistake not, was the first of the class of inn room presidents. The *pro tem* dignity of the president's chair gives its possessor a decision of manner which is quite miraculous to the possessor himself. It is a beautiful sight to see the quiet unpretending man, who all the morning gently insinuates his wishes into the waiter's ear, suddenly transformed by his official honours into a brow-beating man of authority." In this wise does the youthful aspirant become aware of the possible distinction to which he may one day attain.

But it is not in such details as these that the veteran is most interesting in view of the purpose in hand. Rather is one affected towards him because of some other old-fashioned associations that belong to him. He writes of the days before railways, and he calls himself a highwayman because his travels were pursued only along the highways. He belongs to the days of gigs and coaches, and his hints to the youthful traveller reflect those conditions of movement. Fashions, new or old are, however, all relative, and this veteran, old-fashioned to us had a predecessor, who to him was old-fashioned. Writing of the changes which he has observed, he tells of the disappearance of the traveller who moved about on horseback accompanied by his saddle-bags. Of him in contrast to the gig-man he says: "The traveller of the year 1837, and the *Rider* of 1787, are as distinct bipeds as can possibly be classified in the same genus. Their names are not more altered. The old English rider scarcely exists but in tradition. When we have by rare fortune encountered one of these remnants of antiquity, with what reverential curiosity have we noted the time-honoured relic! . . . How have we pondered with upraised hands upon his historical records of the olden times—when without the modern paraphernalia of gigs and mackintoshes, but mounted on his stout and sleek palfrey, almost enveloped by saddle-bags of giant mould, he would issue forth upon an excursion of peril and adventure, cheered on his pilgrimage by the beacon of profit."

When the veteran comes to discourse of the modes of conveyance in vogue in his time he discusses the pros and cons of gig and coach travelling, and advises his youthful friend as to the conditions under which it is best to adopt the one or the other. "Each mode of travel," he says, "has its pleasures and its inconveniences. . . . Among the miseries of commercial life, we may instance the one of rising at three o'clock on an inclement winter morning, or haply sitting up till that time in a cold, solitary bar, amid the perfume of expiring candles. In the one case, you are rudely disturbed from your first slumber by a 'boots,' rendered ferocious by his own sense of the hardship; dress yourself by the aid of a taper which each gust through the ill-fitted window threatens to extinguish, and then groping your way to the cheerless room below, await in shivering durance the arrival of the coach. In some half hour you hear the faint wail of the guard's horn, mingling its tones with the still louder tempest; then you are aware of the fresh horses slowly trailing down to the gateway. Having wound yourself up to a desperate effort, you rush out, and when half recovered from the first blinding gust of sleet and rain, you have the satisfaction of finding the coach full inside and out. You then return to your room with a pleasing sense of the futility of your efforts, and indulge in the agreeable certainty of having to pay for a chaise and pair a few hours later in the morning. All this is avoided by a gig, but gigs are only beneficial when you take small as well as large towns. The expense of either mode of travelling is pretty much the same." As a gig-man, he says, "When you drive into an inn yard, you will generally hear your welcome sounded by a large bell, which is put in motion by some unseen hand in the house itself. This brings the hostler from his stable, and the boots from his kennel; you give your reins and horse to the former, and your luggage to the latter, having first acquainted him with the geography of the packing receptacles of your gig." Here, in the inn yard, as he passes through the portals of his much-desired hostelry to be received there, doubtless, as an honoured and accustomed guest, we must take our leave of the "Veteran Highwayman."

IV.

A Book of Rhymes.

OTHER attractive samples of a prose kind claim one's attention, but they must be regretfully set aside, and one's recreations in this special direction brought to a close by a very brief consideration of the Commercial Traveller as Rhymester. The neat little volume in which this is exemplified is entitled "The Commercial Room, by 'One of Us.'" It is undated, but apparently was published about fifty years ago. It has a pictorial and artistic title-page of the lithographic kind showing the interior of a commercial room, with the various occupants characteristically delineated, and outside this, in illustration of the road-life of the traveller, we have sketches of the gay gig-man of commerce with his high-stepping steed, and the cloaked and top-booted bagman—the antique rider—passing along on his cantering cob.

In the introduction to this book, the rhymester explains his position to his fellows, and, as it were, presents his credentials. He says:

> In making your "*Body*" a subject of song,
> It's right you should know that to it I belong,
> "*Commercial*," I am—"*One of us*,"—"on the *Road*;"
> Your Room is my home, an Hotel my abode.

Then, when he has solemnly invoked his muse, after the manner of the serious poets, we have this response—

> My muse in song would fain describe
> Brothers your *Body* as a tribe,
> *Riders*, were erst your names I'm told,
> A title now that's deem'd too old;
> But whether you on *saddles* ride,
> Or o'er the land on railroads glide,
> Or drive *your own* to cut a show
> In gig the fast, or four-wheel slow.
>
> Your avocation's still the same
> Whatever we may call your name;
> A rose as Shakespeare says so featly,
> By other name would smell as sweetly.
> You are a roving, trav'ling race,
> Who move about from place to place,
> Orders seeking, money taking,
> Albeit few their fortunes making.

Thus does he go on, in a playfully-humorous and sometimes satirical fashion, to describe the traveller's life in his inn rooms, and on the road, presenting us with many sketches of character upon which one may not dwell here. Light and trifling for the most part, his jingling rhymes, plentifully besprinkled with italics, are only interesting to us now as reflecting certain bygone and old-fashioned conditions of travel which are, perhaps, best embodied in a commercial room song—with the music attached to it—which crops up in the course of his narrative. It is in praise of the traveller's life in the driving days and is to this effect:

> A Traveller's life's the best that's led!
> With cob-built tit quite three parts bred—
> Straight back—deep chest—large ears—small head,
> Oh give me the road—the road—the road!
> For the Traveller's life's the best that's led.

after particularising the desirable points of his horse he goes on to say—

> With such a tit, no blemish known—
> His colour bay, black, gray, or roan;
> In dog-cart light—and all my own—
> Oh give me the road—the road—the road!
>
> . . . . .
>
> From all bad debts my ledger freed,
> A trade that would few samples need
> And orders plenty, then I'd lead
> The life of the road—the road—the road!
>
> With these combined, give me the road—
> A Traveller's room my sole abode,
> An inn my house—my life the road.
> Oh give me the road—the road—the road!

Our commercial of this type, like Shenstone's traveller, evidently "found life's warmest welcome at an inn." Apropos of those old riders and gig-men one may fittingly conclude these samples by quoting some lines from another old song of the road contained in a frayed sheet of music of uncertain date,—written after the manner of "The Fine Old English Gentleman,"—they run thus:

> I'll sing you a new song—that I've written now of late,
> Of an old Commercial Traveller—who travelled at slow rate,
> With top-boots, spurs, and saddle-bags—and coat of pompous state,
> He travell'd slow but very sure—and never travell'd late,
> For he was a steady Traveller—one of the olden school.
>
> His horse was short—was stout and strong—and clothed with shaggy hair,
> And though but fourteen hands in height—to see her trot—you'd stare,
> And wonder who the man could be that rode so good a mare,
> Stopping at any road-side Inn—content with humble fare,
> Like a good Commercial Traveller—one of the olden school.
>
> . . . . . .
>
> Unlike the youths who travel now—with cloaks bedeck'd with fur
> And horse that's nearly thorough-bred—and bull or terrier cur,
> And chaise or Stanhope nicely hung—till night they now defer,
> And from the dread to leave their bed—to travel late prefer,
> Like a gay Commercial Traveller—one of the modern school.

IN THE NORTH COUNTRY.

KIRKBY STEPHEN, BARNARD CASTLE, RICHMOND.

I KNOW of nothing more delightful in travel than the sensation one has in fine weather on the threshold of a journey, when all that is before one is new and fresh and full of the anticipation of untasted pleasures. As I stepped out of the train at Kirkby Stephen into the bright sunshine and the sweet air of the fells, and there on the railway platform strapped on my knapsack I felt that in taking on my shoulders that congenial load I had cast off the burden of a year's work. When the train, leaving me standing in the station, had rattled on its way to merry Carlisle, I could see, looking down from the fell side, the pleasant grey town lying below, with the square-towered church dominating it, and beyond these, far away over the dale to distant Stainmoor and the fells across which my road lay. A very inviting country it looked, full of pleasant possibilities, as all hill prospects are, with the vague sense of the unknown lying beyond, that mystery and charm of the land that lies very far off. The polite railway officials could give me little information regarding the road I wished to go, or of Bowes, my first halting-place. It was a long way to drive they said; to walk there seeming to the railway mind an unusual and unnecessary thing.

Kirkby Stephen is beautifully placed in the corner of a hill-bordered vale, with Wild Boar Fell looking down upon it, and the river Eden flowing by. The little town, of Saxon origin, consists mainly of one old-fashioned, oddly-built street, which widens out irregularly to where the ancient church, dedicated to St. Stephen, stands somewhat raised above the rest of the buildings and mainly hid by them, and having a quaint piazza-like market house, otherwise known as the cloister, standing like a gate to a graveyard. The spacious market place is famous for its cattle fairs, and is reminiscent of a form of barter in the exchange of horses. From a tall, russet-clad dalesman in charge of a horse and cart, and attended by a restless, barking sheep dog, I learned that the distance to Bowes was about fifteen miles, and that "t' fells would tak a good deal o' climmin." As he gave me instructions how to thread my way among cross roads, I thought I saw in the eye of that dalesman, as I had in others, a sense of wonder that any one should put a burden on his back and take to tramping along this road for pleasure. Halting once at an inn in Nottinghamshire on my way to merry Sherwood, the landlord, looking with the same wondering eye upon his knapsack-bearing guest, informed me that this sort of exercise reminded him of nothing so much as a species of hard labour, known as pack drill, imposed upon the refractory in a certain prison of which he had been a warder.

From Kirkby Stephen my way lay through a rich belt of pastoral country, well timbered, with clear shining water in the brooks and streams, past the silent hamlet of Winton, hiding itself away from the main road, a cluster of low roofs visible there among the greenery; then through Kaber, with a few cottages and a schoolhouse scattered widely at the foot of the grassy hillside about a spacious green, where the children and geese have it all their own way; then to the pastures of the fell side, broken with copsewood, with the moorland lying above—

Stainmoor's shapeless swell,
And Lunedale wild and Kelton fell,
And rock-begirdled Gilmauscar,
And Arkingdale lay dark afar.

This ridge of fells, scarred by screes and grooved into dales, where among other streams the Lune and the Greta have their sources, was once divided into three great tracts known yet as the forests of Arkingarth, Lune, and Stainmoor. It was towards Stainmoor that I walked, and associated with it came the words of a ballad, which tells how—

> Allen-a-Dale was ne'er belted a knight,
> Though his spur be as sharp, and his blade be as bright;
> Allen-a-Dale is no baron or lord,
> Yet twenty tall yeomen will draw at his word;
> And the best of our nobles his bonnet will vail,
> Who at Rere Cross on Stanmore meets Allen-a-Dale.

There it lay before me in long, waving undulations of rough pasture and brown moorland, with Rere Cross still to be found on it—the cross of kings, ancient boundary mark of kingdoms, rallying point, or for whatever other use set up let antiquarians decide,— interesting only to me at the time in its shadowy association with that forest rover bold Allen-a-Dale. It must be confessed that it was a sad falling off from the purpose of the journey that on the edge of Stainmoor I should find myself constrained from various causes to avail myself of the assistance of a railway train to take me across the forest, but so it was. The autumn afternoon was wearing on, Bowes had to be seen and Barnard Castle reached the same night, and so, with a reluctance almost amounting to a sense of shame, I waited for the train at the fell-side station of Barras, from which high point I could look out over the dale by which I had come and see far away in the dim distance the summits of Saddleback and Helvellyn. The railway runs by steep gradients between Greta beck and the road, with the moorland lying on each side wild and wide open to the air, and dotted here and there with lonesome, desolate-looking homesteads.

Bowes is a hard-featured little town on the edge of Stainmoor, with a single street of grey old houses battered and time-stained, an ancient, barn-like little church topped with a bell turret, and not far away the ruins of the castle-keep standing back from the street on the edge of a pastured slope, with the Greta running through a wooded hollow below.

The Norman Castle of Bowes, built by Alan, first Earl of Richmond, is close by the church, and the land shelves away from it, with the limestone cropping out, down through the meads to the river and the belt of woodland which borders it; and, rising again beyond, shows far-reaching uplands, pale pastured, and darkened here and there with clumps of trees. I strolled down to an old mill on the Greta, and had a chat with the miller's wife about the picturesque features of the place. She told me that the natural arch of limestone rock, known as "God's Bridge," was two miles up the stream, so to see that was, for me, out of the question. She showed me a covered way from the river, which was supposed to communicate with the castle on the hill behind. Her husband had explored it for some distance, but candles or courage failing the end had not been reached. The good dame had an eye for natural beauty, and took me to look at the weir and a stretch of the river behind the mill,

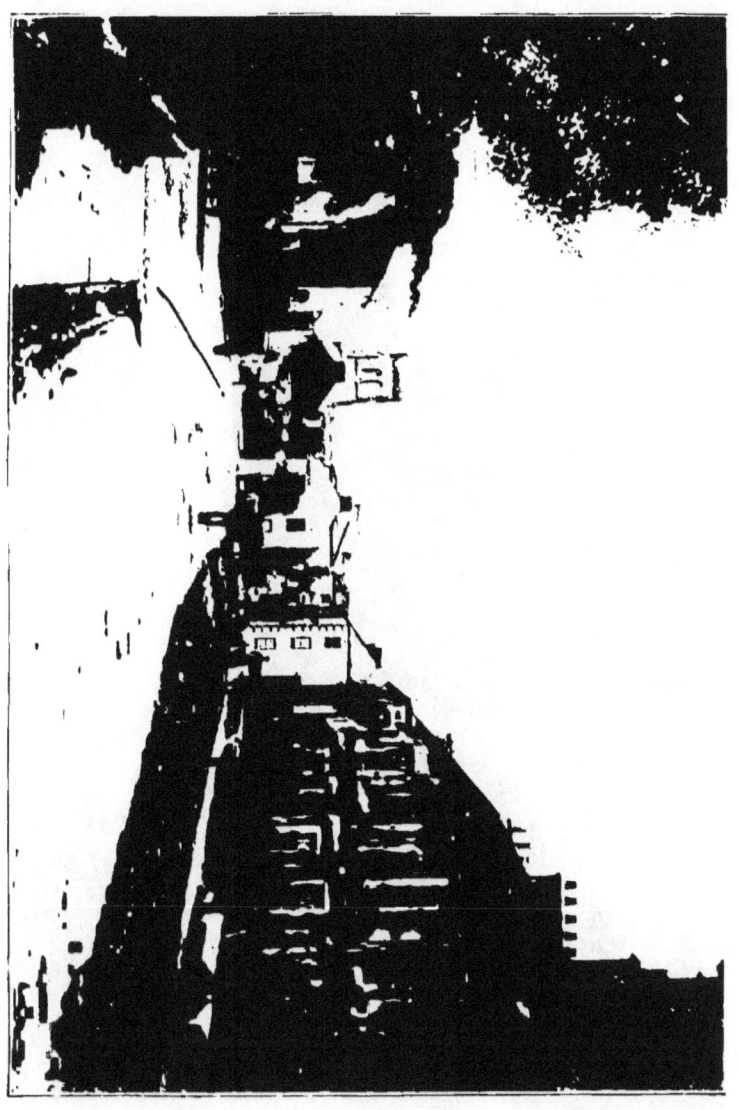

KIRKBY STEPHEN.

BARNARD CASTLE.

which, she said, were the prettiest things to be seen in the neighbourhood. The waterfall, she said, was most beautiful in winter when it was ice-bound and fringed with icicles. While we were talking, the valley, and all the fells were filled and flooded with rose light from the west, and in the glow of it I took my departure for Barnard Castle, stopping on the way to look at the remains of a Roman bath in one of the mill fields—a relic among many of the Roman camp once existing here.

The sunset that flushed the wide landscape must, from Barnard Castle, have resembled in some degree that described in *Rokeby*:—

> The western hills have hid the sun,
> But mountain peak and village spire
> Retain reflection of his fire.
> Old Barnard's towers are purple still,
> To those that gaze from Toller-Hill ;
> Distant and high, the tower of Bowes
> Like steel upon the anvil glows ;
> And Stanmore's ridge, behind that lay
> Rich with the spoils of parting day,
> In crimson and in gold arrayed,
> Streaks yet awhile the closing shade,
> Then slow resigns to darkening heaven
> The tints which brighter hours had given.

It was quite dark when, after walking four or five miles, I came by a sudden descent of the road to the narrow valley or defile through which the Tees flows, and saw the lights of Barnard Castle twinkle like fire-flies on the opposite steep bank of the river. As I crossed the bridge I could see, looming up in the darkness, the shattered walls of the castle crowning the steep scar in front, and could hear the swirl of the water flowing darkly below over the rocky river bed. It is more impressive to enter Barnard Castle in this way than in the daylight. The darkness shuts out or modifies objects that mar the scene, and the doubtful aspect of things helps to favour the illusion that the traveller has lighted upon one of the shores of old romance. There is but one way from this side into Barnard Castle, and it is across the bridge and by a narrow, dimly-lighted street of old houses which winds round to the top of the Scar and brings the traveller out in the market place.

My inn was in the market place, and is associated with Dickens and *Nicholas Nickleby*, and through that book, with a certain Mr. Newman Noggs, who said he was known there. From my bedroom window, looking out in the early morning at the old-fashioned shops on the other side of the market place, I noticed one immediately opposite, owned by a clockmaker, with a clock in the doorway, and above it the name of Humphreys, so to think of *Master Humphrey's Clock* was a natural consequence. Whether the appellation was suggested to Dickens in this way I know not, though some people have said so.

Though Barnard Castle in the daylight had lost some of the air of romantic interest, it still remained attractive. Galgate and the market place

MARKET PLACE, BARNARD CASTLE.

are wide, and in the latter there is an old town hall in the open space with a piazza running round it. The church is an embattled one, Norman, but restored; the shops, as I have said, are quaint, and most of them have small windows. One butcher's shop I saw made quite attractive with flowers and ferns. I rambled to the castle, and descended by the footpath which winds round the walls by the precipitous rocky front of the Scar down to the river. The walls towered and turreted, are of vast dimensions; and on the slope beneath there are cottages with gardens and fruit trees. Opposite the castle is a mill, with a tall chimney. Like Past and Present, the castle and the mill stand face to face, and the river, older than both, flows between. The castle, a stronghold and place of refuge in the disturbed border days, was built by the Balliols, who gave kings to Scotland and a college to Oxford, and became extinct. No words are better than those of a note in Scott's *Rokeby* to describe the outlook from the Scar: "The view from Barnard Castle commands the rich and magnificent valley of the Tees. Immediately adjacent to the river the banks are very thickly wooded; at a little distance they are more open and cultivated, but being interspersed with hedgerows and isolated trees of great age and size, they still retain the richness of wooded scenery. The river itself flows in a deep trench of rock, chiefly limestone and marble."

It is a pleasant walk along the mains, or high pastures, on the Durham side of the Tees, and commands beautiful views of the river below and of Eggleston or Athelstan Abbey on the Yorkshire side, the subject of a stirring scene in *Rokeby*. I crossed the river at Abbey Bridge, and saw from it some of the finest stream scenery of its kind I have ever looked upon. The river flows over slabs of grey marble through a ravine or defile thickly clothed with trees to the water's edge. The bridge spans this at a great height, and commands long views between the wooded slopes, taking in Athelstan Abbey, and extending from Barnard Castle to Rokeby Hall, which is seen perched high among the trees at the end of the long avenue of the river. I went down to the stream and followed the path by the side of it, among the rocks and trees and past the flowing water, in which stood a solitary angler casting his fly, and for once realised that I was in a romance country full of charming possibilities for poet and painter. I left the river at Rokeby Park and went past the front of the hall to Greta Bridge close by. It is not easy to describe the beauties of Rokeby, Scott has done it in verse, and it is needless that I should attempt to do so lamely in prose. It is made up of parklands, meads and pastures, thick woods, tree-shaded roads, moss-grown walls, a hamlet of straggling houses with a grey antiquity about them, and a reposeful calm over all, save where the fretful

Greta hurries over its stony bed through the woodland to join the Tees in Rokeby Park. I rested for awhile at the Morritt Arms, where a guide is provided and permission given to see the more secluded parts of Rokeby Park. The guide was a courteous veteran soldier, who had lost an arm and wore Indian medals on his breast, but there were yet ten miles of road to travel before Richmond could be reached. So I departed with a mental resolve that some day, the mood serving, I would come again and avail myself of that guide, and see Rokeby in the way that an orthodox tourist should.

I passed out over the Greta Bridge and by a group of buildings which formed the famous old posting-house, known in *Nicholas Nickleby* as the George and New Inn, a stirring place in the coaching days on this main north road, with rambling stables and out-houses about it, and the open grass-grown space in front where the horses where changed. Then through a high country, with the sunlight shining on it and a bracing wind blowing over it, I went, sometimes loitering by the wayside or lying lazily upon the broad ledge of a bridge to listen to the murmur of the water and look up into the tree tops and the pleasant sky, and watch the flight of birds. Once, after climbing the steep road, I rested to drink from a runlet of water that came down from the moorlands, a fitting place to halt, for below me were the ruins of Ravensworth Castle, and behind the forest of Arkindale. While I sat watching a bee trying to bury itself head downwards in the delicate green moss that had gathered in the trough into which the runlet leaped, there came a peasant to get water there with whom I had some pleasant wayside gossip, and who, among other things, told me a weird story of a local kind, the incidents of which, however, are too modern for repetition here.

The ancient church of Kirkby Ravensworth stands upon a hill, and commands fine views of the dales. The old men of the village were seated sunning themselves against the churchyard wall as I passed on my way to Richmond. As I climbed the wooded heights by the steep road I met the good folks coming home from market on horseback, in gigs, and on foot. "The castle of Richmond stands fair on the hill," says the ballad; but you look down on it as you approach it from this road, and can scarcely realise that the town is built on several small hills, with the castle standing on a rugged promontory of rock rising high above the river. A sentinel was pacing before a barrack gate, and an artist was planted in the road with his camp-stool, sketching, as I dropped down to the old town, which showed a group of clustered roofs and gables, with the walls of the castle-keep and the beautiful ruined tower of Grey Friars rising above them, and the broad and silent dales stretching out far below. Like all Yorkshire agricultural towns Richmond is

RICHMOND, YORKSHIRE.

MARKET PLACE, RICHMOND.

neat and clean, and as far as my experience goes it is one of the most picturesque in the county. I took up my quarters at the King's Head, which stands at an angle of the wide market place. Opposite to the hotel, at another angle of the market place, is an ancient church, still used for divine service, with old-fashioned shops clinging to it like barnacles.

For awhile I lounged about the town of Richmond, descended to the river, and ascended by the steep pathway to the rocky promontory, where, high above the Swale and its wooded shores, stand the vast ruins of the fortress of Alan the Norman, first Earl of Richmond, not altogether unused in this day, but for the most part roofed, like Allen-a-Dale's forest hall, "with the blue vault of heaven." The castle has a history which I have not space to dwell upon, and it has also a legend. In Brittany the people used to sing, "King Arthur is not dead, Arthur will come again;" and in Sir Thomas Malory's *Morte d'Arthur* we read that "Some men yet sing in many parts of England that King Arthur is not dead. . . . . And men say that he will come again." Now some men have said that Arthur sleeps an enchanted sleep with his knights in a cave of this castle of Richmond. A sword and a horn lie by the sleepers, and whoever blows the horn or draws the sword will wake them, to the help of England and to the performance of noble deeds.

A DAY AT DERBY.

THE traveller from Manchester to Derby who journeys by one of the Midland London or West of England express trains, from the Central Station, is timed to arrive in the central midland town in less than an hour and a half. When Bonnie Prince Charlie, in 1745, marched the same distance with his army, having along with his Highlanders a certain ill-fated Manchester regiment, it took four days to accomplish that futile errand—but that is another story. Derby is a little more than sixty miles away from Cottonopolis, and between the two places the railway traverses a delightful and varied breadth of country, whose most picturesque features are arrived at through graduated stages. As soon as you have glided clear of the belt of dim streets and of smoke-haunted roofs bristling here and there with tall factory chimneys, getting on your way glimpses of inky Irwell and the Ship Canal beyond, you emerge into the green surroundings of a flat landscape and pass by farm and field, and through stations bearing the names of villages which are now developing into great communities, the suburban refuges of town-wearied men. So do you reach Stockport, hazy with smoke of factories, but not altogether unpicturesque in its situation, seen there spreading itself irregularly on many slopes and deep-indented where the Mersey flows through a rocky channel of red-sandstone. Beyond this you are carried by ascending gradients to the hill country, and through a portion of the Cheshire Highlands, with Werneth Low on your left as you cross the lofty viaduct which spans the wooded gorge lying between Romiley and Marple. Thence do you pass into the Strines valley, watered by the river Goyt, and notable for a great printworks located there, showing many whitened walls among the green meadow spaces. With Cobden Edge and other moorland heights in view you come to New Mills whose factories have now grown old, and are seen rising from the rock ledges of deeply-quarried chasms that must at one time have appeared romantic. Then as you rattle along over the Bugsworth viaduct and so to Chapel-en-le-Frith, you have Eccles Pike, cone-shaped, on the one hand, and on the other, over lower hills, you get sight of the rocky ridge of Kinder Scout. You are now in one of the gateways of the Peak, and between the green pastured slopes your train carries you upwards to the Dove

Holes hill and into the long tunnel there, from which you come out into a land of limestone, green-turfed in many undulations, and streaked with grey stone walls, the first station you pass being that lime-dusted one known as Peak Forest. As you rush along through

NEAR MILLER'S DALE.

deep cuttings where lime is being quarried or burnt in smoking kilns, the country becomes more picturesque with crag and tor, feathery woodland, and boulder-strewn stream, reaching its climax of beauty as you pass through the dales of Miller and Monsall, with the Wye winding in and out there in close companionship.

MARKET PLACE, DERBY.

After passing Bakewell greyly-grouped in a green hollow, you see the stream in more sylvan surroundings, meandering through the beautiful vale towards Haddon Hall. That romantic old house is not visible, but instead you find yourself rumbling through a tunnel almost immediately underneath it, and which bears its name. At Rowsley, with its old fishing hostelry, mullioned and gabled, you are where the Wye falls into the Derwent, a stream which is more or less in evidence until you reach your destination. Through wooded vales and the dale of Darley, you speed towards Matlock Bridge and Matlock Bath, getting glimpses of whitened roads and white houses, grouped beneath overhanging tors, that are tree-belted, rugged and craggy. Then you pass Cromford, and after that Whatstandwell, where road, railway, canal and river run side by side in the contracted space, and so to Ambergate Junction, with opening valleys to right and left, and with the lofty hill of Crich near by. Belper, with its famous mills among green surroundings by Derwent side, is passed in rapid flight, and then through cutting and tunnel you run into the wider valley of the Derwent, and amid scenery of a more pastoral kind, until the spires and towers of Derby come in sight, and you are set down at the great Midland Station there.

Your first impression is that you have been set down in a region of railway offices, sheds and workshops which surround you on every hand and stretch out beyond the station area. That you have arrived at a centre of great activity and that this vast railway depôt is a dominating feature in the life of the Derby of to-day will be made apparent when you come to know, as you may do later, the nature and extent of the work that is going on here. Meanwhile the town claims your first attention, and that in the oldest part, though linked continuously with its great station, lies some distance away. A tram-car will take you to the market place, but the more leisurely observer may prefer to walk. The main avenue of approach on this side is along the London road, which has trees in it, with installations of the electric light budding out from among them. Here, too, you pass the new Infirmary, with buildings of roseate hue standing among green interspaces; opposite to it is another harbour of refuge in the form of the Liversage almshouses, not lacking in touches of quaintness and an air of quiet restfulness. As you proceed you find yourself among converging streets of varying gradients, indicating the unequal surface upon which the town has laid its foundations. In these thoroughfares, some of which are known as "gates," the shops and other edifices are often of a solid and handsome kind, and along the footways there is a cheerful market-day activity. The market place is a spacious and many-stalled area, suggestive in some of its features of the old county town conditions. Some of the buildings, we are told, were once the residences of noble families, and here, too, is an old Assembly room, with its own associations of social festivity. The Town Hall is the most prominent feature, with its Guildhall chamber and clock tower, beneath which, through an archway, you may pass to a great market hall in the rear. Rising behind the open area in one direction is a shot tower, and in another the beautiful traceried and pinnacled tower of All Saints' Church, of which the Derby people are very proud.

In this open market place it may be fitting to pause for awhile and indulge in a little historical retrospection. Derby is a very old town, with a very dim, far-off origin. The borough arms show "a buck couchant in a park," a suggestive feature, but not sufficient, a local historian says, to indicate clearly how the town got its name. The Saxons and the Danes, who fought with each other for foothold here, knew it by a name which signified the northern market, and also as *Deoraby*, the abode of deer. There are other suggestions connecting it with the river Derwent, but "the buck in the park" has pleasant greenwood associations and may suffice. As a tavern sign it is pictorial, and the Midland Railway people have given it an honoured place in their armorial emblazonments. We are told that the Saxons minted money here, and that the town sent bowmen to the battle of Hastings. It has had royal visitations, and also a gruesome one when the plague found its way here in 1665. At that time, old Hutton says "the town was forsaken, the farmers declined the market place, and grass grew upon the spot which had furnished the supports of life." Instead the farmers and the town's folk made use of a Headless Cross, at which, with due precautions against touch and with purification of coin by the aid of vinegar, exchanges were made. Other chronicles there are not to be set down here, but to a visitor from Cottonopolis, the coming hither of Prince Charlie and his followers in the memorable '45, is an interesting incident. They arrived here on the 4th of December, and on the following day "the Highlanders were to be seen during the whole day in crowds before the shops of the cutlers quarrelling about who should be the first to sharpen and give a proper edge to their swords." It was a needless preparation, for ere another day had passed the retreat was sounded, and on the ninth the Prince and his army were in Manchester again *en route* for Scotland.

When you leave the market place the town "is all before you where to choose." From the higher levels you may get glimpses of its surroundings, and see in what a pleasant vale it is placed. In your wanderings you may come upon old mansions and old gardens, and if you are interested in old churches they are here for your inspection, and in the near neighbourhood of some of these you may find quiet nooks and corners

ON THE DERWENT, OLD SILK MILL, DERBY.

wherein you may loiter. Byeways of this kind there are about the church of All Saints', whose beautiful Gothic tower is so inconsistent with the remainder of the architecture. Here is the monument of "Bess of Hardwick," and here lie many noble members of the house of Cavendish. Near by you may come upon some forlorn and deserted almshouses which were founded by that remarkable lady.

Derby can scarcely be reckoned among large textile manufacturing towns as we know them now, but it is not without its important industries, and the tall chimney crops out here and there above the roofs. In the old days it had its merchant guild and a monopoly of dyeing cloth. In later times it has dealt with silk in various forms. If you go down to the Derwent you will see there a large silk mill, associated retrospectively with an older one, which had the reputation of being the first of its kind erected in England. The date of its foundation was 1718, and the story of its origin is interesting. We are told that "in the early part of the eighteenth century the Italians exclusively possessed the art of spinning, or as it is technically called 'throwing' silk, and the British weaver had to import thrown silk at an exorbitant price. In 1717 Mr. John Lombe, who had in disguise and by bribing the workmen, obtained access to the machinery of the silk throwsters of Piedmont, agreed with the corporation of Derby to rent, on a long lease, for £8 a year an island or swamp in the river Derwent, 500 feet long and 52 feet wide. Here he erected at a cost of £30,000 an immense silk mill. The foundation was formed with oaken piles 16 to 20 feet long, and over this mass of timber was laid a foundation of stone, on which were turned stone arches that support the walls." We are further told that Lombe took out his patent and was working successfully when he suddenly died under circumstances that were accounted mysterious. In addition to silk mills, the town has its iron foundries, paper mills, malting houses, tanneries, coachbuilding works, and works of other kinds, but it is in connection with the potter's craft in its fine artistic expression that the name of Derby is for some people more closely associated—as everyone knows it has its own special reputation for the manufacture of porcelain—and "Crown Derby" has become a household name among lovers of choice china. The history of the old Derby china factory has been written, and it is a very interesting story. Therein may you learn how William Duesbury, in 1750, came to the town, and began to mould clay in beautiful forms, and how he and other Duesburys who succeeded him, together with many clever workmen, developed their craft in the directions of texture, colour, design, and other artistic ways until they made their productions famous. If you are interested in those old specimens of ceramic art, you cannot do better than visit the Free

ALL SAINTS' CHURCH, DERBY.
(From a Photograph by Messrs. F. Frith & Co. Ltd. By permission.)

Library and Museum, a handsome building in the Flemish-Gothic style, and there you will see a fine collection of old Derby china, the work of the Duesburys and others. Then if you wish to know under what conditions "Crown Derby" is produced in these days, you may acquire such knowledge by visiting the Royal Porcelain Works, pleasantly placed and garden-fronted, and with the Arboretum in the rear. Then again, when you have had enough of art you may stroll into this Arboretum, and wander along its pleasant green alleys and see preserved there the Headless Cross or plague stone, of which mention has already been made.

What the old county town was like in the drowsy days of the stage coaches and postchaises must be left to the imagination working upon such materials as still survive. With the advent of the "kettle o' steam" a change came o'er the spirit of its dream, and to-day its interests and prosperity are bound up with those of a great railway company. A visit to Derby, though transitory, would be incomplete without some impression being gained of this aspect of its affairs. The history of the Midland Railway is contained in a bulky volume. From that source you may learn that the system, which has now become so vast, was not cradled here, but had its birthplace in a little village inn in Nottinghamshire, where, in 1832, some local coal-owners were seated in conference round a parlour table.

The line of railway they were considering was a local one, and had mainly to do with the carriage of coals, but in what they were projecting existed the germ of subsequent developments. In the nebulous period Derby exercised an attractive and centralising influence, and if you look at a railway map you will see, in the radiation of lines that run from the town, to what an extent this centralising influence has made itself manifest. Among the early incidents in the story of growth is a description of old George Stephenson, accompanied by his secretary, starting out in a yellow postchaise from the New Inn at Derby, to find the best route for a line to connect that town with Leeds. About the same time there was a proposition set on foot for running a line between Derby and Birmingham, "old George" being in this case also the engineer. The projectors of these enterprises were for the most part outsiders. When a deputation came from Birmingham to appeal to the inhabitants of Derby for support, they called a public meeting to be held in the hotel in which they were staying. After dinner they sent to the adjoining room to see how many had responded, and the messenger reported that three persons were present; after waiting another half hour the messenger was sent again, and came back with the news that a dozen people had arrived on the scene. At this period, we are told, "the folding doors that separated the dining room and the hall were now withdrawn. The deputation, with all the dignity they could muster, advanced to the platform, and proceeded to unfold their budget to the twelve men of Derby." The audience, however, though few, was found to be fit, and the enterprise was proceeded with. An incident of this kind is interesting in view of the present conditions. In Derby the Midland Railway Company has found its most fitting centre. Here it has its works of construction and its offices for the administration of its affairs. Of the magnitude of these operations you may, with due permission obtained, acquire some little knowledge.

Presenting yourself in the proper official quarter, the first courteous response to your enquiry is in the form of a slip of printed matter bristling with figures and giving you a sort of synopsis of the system, based upon the previous year's working. From this, primarily, you learn that the expended capital has exceeded ninety-six millions sterling, that the working expenses, salaries, and wages have been in excess of nine millions, that there are over fifty-six thousand men employed, that more than forty-three million passengers have been conveyed, and that the trains have covered in their running nearly forty-two millions of miles. Though valuable in other ways, it would be tedious to detail here all the information thus presented, but it is interesting to learn, concerning Derby, that the clerical staff there numbers two thousand three hundred persons, and that there are ten thousand men employed upon the works. With a deep though confused sense of the importance of the statistics you have been considering, you now start out on a brief tour of survey, and are first conducted along an elevated way which crosses the station to the locomotive works. These, with their sheds and open spaces intersected by railway lines, occupy an area of eighty acres. The engines of the company dealt with here in construction and repair exceed in number two thousand four hundred, and over four thousand workmen are employed upon them, among whom, in wages, an amount of more than five thousand pounds is distributed weekly. One of the first things shown you here is the provision made for the comfort of the workmen in the form of three large dining halls or mess rooms, fitted up in a neat and atractive form with every required convenience. If the object of your visit is to see, in detail, how a locomotive is built, your stay will be a prolonged one, otherwise you must be content with a general, if vague impression. To this end you pass from one vast workshop to another, seeing first a great smithy with fifty fires aglow, and then follow your conductor through wheel-turning shops, spring shops, boiler shops, and numerous other shops, with all about you the sound of hammers wielded by hand or worked by steam, the whirl of wheels, and much other clatter and din of machinery. It is at best perplexing to the outsider this multifarious and multitudinous series of operations. You recognise in a dim way that wheels, axles, cylinders, cranks, boilers and other component parts of a locomotive are being evolved from apparently chaotic conditions. But it is "toil cooperate to an end," as you begin to realise when you approach the completer forms as displayed in the erecting shops, and see your engine taking recognisable shape. The illustration here given will suit better than any word description. It is an impressive sight these rows of powerful locomotives standing on their rails above the hollow ways. Some of them are new, others are here for repairs. If you should wonder how they are dealt with in the matter of lifting when displacement is necessary, a great travelling crane above will afford the explanation. This is capable of lifting an engine of sixty tons weight with perfect ease, and will convey it clear of the rest to any required place on the rails. One noticeable feature of these engines of the Midland Company, with their familiar colouring of crimson lake, is that they are not named but numbered, a form of identification which seems lacking in sentiment. To confer a name upon an engine is to give it a kind of personal individuality, otherwise it is only one of a series of similar mechanisms. When you have wandered through these shops and foundries, and your hour of inspection is nearly completed, it remains but to see the ring sheds where, among radiating lines and turn-tables, the engines are "stabled" in their intervals of work, and here you find that accommodation is provided for one hundred and fifty of them, where they may cool themselves after heated work, be cleaned and prepared for further duty.

It is now time to depart to the carriage building works, which lie half a mile away to the south, and cover an area of eighty-six acres. In this equally busy region you have a vast number of covered workshops, in which four thousand men are employed. In the locomotive works you were in an arena where metal was most in evidence; here the material is mainly wood. You see trains arriving with loads of timber, and timber in evidence everywhere. You are first taken to the great sawmill, of which an illustration is here given. You see the wood being dealt with by steam saws, and a multitude of other shaping machines. Then you go to the wagon shop and see how a wagon is constructed, and learn that one may be commenced and finished in a day. Further again you proceed to the carriage-building shop and see how a railway carriage is fashioned, and are then introduced to the paint shop, where, among colours, crimson lake has the most honoured place. In their turns you visit the forge shed, a fiery place, where much welding of metal is going on, and where wheels take shape; the smithy and spring shop, where carriage springs are made and subjected to severe testings; and the great machine shop, of which the illustration gives you some impression. In the foreground is a space reserved for those who

MIDLAND RAILWAY WORKS, DERBY.

MIDLAND RAILWAY WORKS, DERBY.
MACHINE SHOP.—*Carriage and Wagon Department.*

MIDLAND RAILWAY WORKS, DERBY.
ERECTING SHOP.—Locomotive Department.

deal with the brass fittings of carriages. Elsewhere you have machinery of the most ingenious and diverse kinds, dealing with other forms of metal work. You see wheels having their tires fixed, axles being fitted therein by hydraulic pressure, and many other operations. Very bald indeed are these references to what is shown you, but detailed description is impossible here. You might spend half a day in one workshop and then leave it unexhausted. As in the case of the locomotives, it is when you are brought to the shed where finished carriages |are standing that your interest culminates. Here you see a row of handsomely painted and varnished vehicles, a break van, an [ordinary carriage, a saloon carriage, and a dining car. The furnishings and appointments are choice and even luxurious. These are not first-class carriages, but will form the third class portion of a train, and are of the latest construction for long-journey express purposes. When you look upon these lofty, roomy, well ventilated, and richly upholstered vehicles, you will, if you are old enough, let your mind travel back to the time when as a third-class railway passenger you had to be content to travel in an open truck, standing therein as only cattle do in these more favoured days. In relation to this carriage-building department you learn that the number of passenger coaches in use is in excess of four thousand one hundred, and that the wagon stock exceeds one hundred and sixteen thousand.

In this connection it may be remarked that the unreflecting outsider is apt to think of railways as existing mainly for the conveyance of passengers, an impression corrected in this case of the Midland by the fact that the revenue from goods, cattle and minerals is more than double that from passenger traffic.

When you have completed your brief survey, and turn to retrace your steps to the station, your eye may light upon a deserted-looking tree-shaded mansion, the outlook from whose windows was once over pleasant parklands or pastures, but is now across the broad verdureless space with its hives of busy workers, and the railed ways where goods trains glide. There is a sharp contrast between this old Osmaston Hall—with its associations of postchaises and stage coaches—and its present surroundings, and so it is with things old and new in your mind that you finish your day at Derby and take train for home.

PREVIOUS TREATISES

By JOHN MORTIMER

(Chief Cashier, Henry Bannerman & Sons Limited, Spinners, Manufacturers and Merchants).

Published in the "DIARY AND BUYERS' GUIDE."

FROM COTTON TO CLOTH.

CALICO PRINTING.

FROM FLEECE TO FLANNEL.

FROM FLAX TO LINEN.

HENRY BANNERMAN AND SONS LIMITED:
ITS ORIGIN, RISE, AND PROGRESS.

HOW A LACE CURTAIN IS MADE.

[OVER.

PREVIOUS TREATISES—*Continued.*

CONCERNING VELVETEEN.

GOLD. * * * A FACTORY TOWN.

COTTON: FROM FIELD TO FACTORY.
A CITY POST OFFICE.

COTTON SPINNING: THE STORY OF THE SPINDLE.

MERCANTILE MANCHESTER: PAST AND PRESENT.

INDUSTRIAL LANCASHIRE.

www.ingramcontent.com/pod-product-compliance
Lightning Source LLC
Chambersburg PA
CBHW021345230426
43666CB00006B/416